remembering paris

other books in the sandra hochman collection
from turner publishing:

Walking Papers

Endangered Species

Happiness Is Too Much Trouble

Jogging

Playing Tahoe

Streams

Loving Robert Lowell

for children:

The Magic Convention

forthcoming:

The Shakespeare Conspiracy

Portraits of Genius Friends

sandra hochman

remembering paris

1958-1960

A Memoir

TURNER

Turner Publishing Company
Nashville, Tennessee
New York, New York

www.turnerpublishing.com

Remembering Paris 1958-1960: A Memoir

Copyright © 2017 Sandra Hochman. All rights reserved.

This book or any part thereof may not be reproduced or transmitted in any form or by any means, electronic or mechanical, including photocopying, recording, or by any information storage and retrieval system, without permission in writing from the publisher.

Cover design: Maddie Cothren
Book design: Glen Edelstein

Library of Congress Cataloging-in-Publication Data

Names: Hochman, Sandra, author.
Title: Remembering Paris : 1958-1960 / Sandra Hochman.
Description: Nashville, Tennessee : Turner Publishing Company, 2017.
Identifiers: LCCN 2017031347 (print) | LCCN 2017038492 (ebook) | ISBN
  9781683365365 (e-book) | ISBN 9781683365341 (pbk.)
Subjects: LCSH: Hochman, Sandra. | Authors, American--Biography.
Classification: LCC PS3558.O34 (ebook) | LCC PS3558.O34 Z46 2017
(print) |
  DDC 813/.54 [B] --dc23
LC record available at https://lccn.loc.gov/2017031347 9781683365341

Printed in the United States of America
17 18 19 20 9 8 7 6 5 4 3 2 1

For Matt Cornell, my friend and a great healer

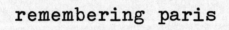

remembering paris

1

Back Story

1957. Again, it was a hated Christmas vacation from college. It was my last year at Bennington. This Christmas, at least I had a new friend. He was the very short, dark-haired, intellectual, handsome Tony Winner, an adjunct professor at Harvard who was writing his doctoral thesis on Dos Passos. We had met during a three month period when I audited classes at Cambridge and had many literary conversations. He invited me to a concert and a party afterward being given by his aunt and uncle, the Sorias, who owned Angel Records in New York City.

At this elegant party, held at the Pierre Hotel in New York, I saw Shomsky for the first time. He was tall and very blond and bohemian. He was only fourteen years older than me, but because he was so sophisticated I thought he looked even older. I was twenty. I didn't care; I thought he was gorgeous. Instead of black tie, he wore a cape and corduroy pants and sandals. He radiated mysterious and charming charisma. A woman was holding his hand.

"Who is that handsome man?" I asked.

"That's Shomsky," said Tony. "He's a great Israeli violinist." He told me that Shomsky was discovered at age twelve, in what was then Palestine, by Bronislaw Huberman, who was on a tour of the Middle East searching for young violin talent. Huberman took Shomsky to Paris, where he studied and began giving concerts at age thirteen. He was called the wunderkind. Soon he became "the rage of Paris." Tony continued talking in his pedantic way as he squeezed my hand: "He concertized all over Europe until the war, when he escaped the Nazis and moved with his mother to London. Now, many years later, he's been making a comeback and has recorded the Berg violin concerto and the Bartók for Vox Records. He's also made an amazing recording of the Stravinsky violin concerto. Stravinsky adores him. So does Heifetz. A lot of people think he's one of the greatest violinists alive, but his career has gone nowhere. My uncle told me he has no management. After the war, he was represented by the great impresario Sol Hurok, but, amazingly, Sol Hurok dropped him. No one knows why, probably too many iconic concert violinists on his list. But the buzz is Shomsky was too temperamental."

I listened breathlessly, trying to find out as much as possible.

At the party, Shomsky smiled at me, and I smiled back at him. I thought he was Byronesque, romantic and handsome in a white-skinned, chiseled way. A few moments later, in the ladies' room, I stood at a sink next to the woman who had been holding his hand. I summoned my courage to find out if this attractive woman who had been clutching his arm was his wife.

"Your husband is very handsome," I said innocently, washing my hands.

"You mean Shomsky? My escort?" She was washing her hands also. I watched soap bubbles rising from her large diamond ring.

"Yes."

She laughed. "He's not my husband. I'm Mrs. Isaac Stern." She said this in a voice of royalty.

I was excited and relieved. He was not married after all. At least I had a chance. He was flirtatious and single. I ran out of the bathroom and right up to this blond stranger. I was wearing a blue and gold off-the-shoulder dress, which the cheapest dressmaker who sold her services to Bennington girls, Miss Tize, had created for me out of a magnificent sari. The sari was given to my father as a gift by an Indian guest, Mr. Parivallah, who stayed at the Dryden, one of my father's two hotels. He paid his rent to my father in precious stones and saris. Shomsky looked straight into my eyes.

"I'm going to marry you," he said.

"You are? Don't you want to know my name first?" I asked, smiling. It was exciting to be addressed this way by a stranger. He obviously had a sense of humor. "In laughter the pain of the heart is eased"—suddenly I remembered the verse from Proverbs 4:13.

"Yes. What is it?"

"Sandra."

"What an original name. And what is your phone number, Sandra?" he asked, still smiling. I told him. "Oregon nine, three nine hundred."

He took a ballpoint pen out of his pocket and wrote my number on the palm of his hand, as if he were tattooing it into his skin.

"I'll call you," he said. "Tomorrow morning."

Mrs. Isaac Stern came out of the ladies' room to claim Shomsky and whisked him off to the buffet table, which was laden with too much food. It was an after-concert party to celebrate the American debut of the great conductor Igor Markevitch, who was now recording for Angel Records.

I stood there smiling and thrilled that this strange and golden violinist wanted to see me again. As if to discourage me, Tony told me how old he was, but I didn't care about the age difference. He had no idea that I was a virgin, knew nothing about sex, and lived practically like a nun. Even if he did know, he wouldn't have cared. He had decided in one moment that I was juicy and he wanted to marry me. It was physical attraction, of course, but it was also his need. He needed someone to share his life, preferably someone pretty and young and American, and he decided in a split second it would be me. The up-and-down dark tunnel inside my body was thrown into light by a slow oxidation. I had suddenly been granted joy, and this new light inside me began to radiate its own energy. It drowned out my sorrow of being alone. My Russian grandmother oncoe whispered to me "Love is need." Was she right?

I only knew that his name was Shomsky and that he was a violinist, and all he knew was that my name was Sandra. And he had my phone number. And that was what made it exciting. We were strangers who were attracted to each other. It crossed my mind that I had found myself flirting with my father's worst nightmare. A foreigner, a concert violinist in a cape, an aging bohemian wearing sandals. My father, dear old bourgeois Daddy, with a daughter who had bizarre ideas of being a poet and even more bizarre ideas of not marrying into wealth. He would have been furious to know I was attracted to a fiddler, an artist, worst of all a gypsy musician.

At my father's hotel that night, I was sleepless. My large bed in the well-furnished penthouse was covered with a colorful chintz spread. At six in the morning, the phone rang.

I was breathless. It was Shomsky. In his French accent he invited me to come and see him immediately. "Come right over. I'm at the Plaza Hotel," he said. "But please don't think I'm a millionaire just because I'm at the Plaza. I'm a penniless violinist who's staying, thank God, in a rich man's suite. Victor Borge, the millionaire Danish comedian-pianist, is my patron, and he puts me up in style in his own empty apartment, where I can't even afford room service." He laughed at his absurd state of poverty.

So what?, I thought. Frankly, I didn't care if he was poor. To me, he was a glamorous and famous international concert artist. That was so seductive, and the fact that he was drop-dead handsome didn't hurt. "Thank you, God," I said silently. I could hardly believe he was interested in me. I was Eve running to meet Adam. I was running to meet Caesar, and I was Cleopatra. I was Sheba running to meet Solomon. I was no longer me; I was a young stupid woman ruled by my glands. I was somebody else, lifted with delirium that was erotic and yet innocent. I had never made love with anyone, and now I was going to the hotel room of this shining stranger. It was dangerous and exciting. I heard strains of the violin in the long, green-carpeted hallway as I ran to the door of his suite.

When he opened the door, he was wearing a white shirt with a hole in it and corduroy pants. He had been practicing the violin. He put the beautiful, polished wooden instrument down as I entered the room. He looked at me and said, "My God, you're young."

I'd never really felt that I was young.

"I am?"

I looked into the mirror, which was actually a wall of mirrors. I saw him, and I saw me. I watched as he came closer to kiss me. I was observing myself as he kissed me for the first time. We were two candles setting the room on fire.

*   *   *

That morning, the first time we made love, we were lying naked on the white Egyptian-cotton sheets that cradled the huge bed. The linens smelled like fresh lavender.

"Oh, Shomsky." I repeated his name over and over as I sucked him into my body with muscles that somehow didn't have to be taught what to do. At first I experienced pain, then pleasure. He had no idea that this was the first time I had ever made love. Bennington girls had a reputation for being fast, but I was not a typical Bennington girl. I was a virgin who wanted to wait, and men didn't interest me as much as literature did. God had told me, I imagined, that I was going to be a poet when I grew up. The idea of being just a housewife revolted me. Nobody ever got an orgasm from washing a floor. So to play it safe, I didn't date anyone. I didn't want to be ordinary, thank you very much. I wanted to be extraordinary. I sensed that Shomsky *was* extraordinary.

On the white sheets of the king-size bed, there were a few drops of blood, which Shomsky didn't notice. I made sure to cover my blood with the huge, starched, white pillow shams.

After we made love, Shomsky picked up his gleaming brown violin and played a few bars from a Bach chaconne. The music was strong, strident, and truly beautiful. Then he put down his violin. "If I can make this old box sound like that, imagine what I could do with a Strad!"

He took me again into his arms. "I need a good woman like you behind me," he said. I had never been called a good woman before. Everything was happening so fast. I was now living in a dream which moved out over the things of the world. A song stuck in my belly, a song that betrayed the fire of my childhood and resonated over the dust of the sea of my unhappiness and rose to my tongue. I kissed him again and again.

6

* * *

In the first few months that I knew him, I was besotted by Shomsky. I went back to Bennington College and couldn't stop talking about him. I had his recordings on the Vox label, which I played all the time in my room to anyone who would listen. I began reading everything I could find about the history of music, the art of the violin, how violins were made, and the lives of all the great violinists. I was obsessed with Shomsky. His face, his name were all over my room. He had given me several promotional glossies from his early Sol Hurok days, and I had them framed and hung them on the walls. My college room looked like a shrine to Shomsky. It was hard to be in love and be me at the same time, so I gave up being me and became totally distracted from my previous passion for literature and poetry. All my ambitions were drowned in a sea of love. I imagined being with Shomsky for the rest of my life. All I could think of was making love and my newfound passion for classical music. I also experienced a vigorous light between my thighs that I hadn't had as a virgin.

In the last part of my senior year, Shomsky and I talked all the time. I used the public phone in the Stokes House dormitory. Without telling my father, I rode down to New York on a bus and stayed with Shomsky at the Plaza. The first night we were together, I read my poems to him, picking out the two that related to Jerusalem and David and Goliath. I told him that he was my David. Goliath was the concert world that I wanted to help him conquer in his comeback so he could be rich and famous again, as he had been when he was a wunderkind.

I read to him in my slightly throaty voice:

THE PROBLEM OF DAVID

He lay with his head filled with psalms,
wondering how a boy

could shed all dreams from his mind
and arise to conquer a giant.
The battle was set for dawn.
All the dark night he lay, facing the stars and his God
    without a plan.
"Visions, am I to die?"
My mind is caught with the tunes
you taught me when I was a child.
They will not let me arm.
How shall I begin to think of the battle?
The way to fight my enemy?
Only these songs
remain to keep me company.
When the army was all arrived,
and Goliath stood in that place where he knew the
    battle would be,
David, armed for the moment of death,
turned all songs into a stone
and overthrew the flesh.

"Oh, I love your words, your images, your magic," he said. "I love that poem. I love it so much! Will you give it to me?" I handed him the neatly typed poem: tore it out of my poetry binder, signed it, and gave it to him. He had tears in his eyes and said, "I promise you I'll put this inside my violin case and carry it with me all over the world." My first gift to him. Was he interested in my poetry, or only in my pussy? I could never tell.

I had no idea about the phony and sycophantic politics of the showbiz concert world. How did a concert violinist get concerts? Shomsky explained that he had to play up to a lot of old ladies who were powerful. In other words, he had to kiss ass to succeed. It was mostly old ladies, he said, who were patrons of music. Enter Mildred Dilling, a red-haired harpist in her sixties. She had yellow buck teeth, dyed hair, and terrible body odor, and she was, Shomsky told me, one of the greatest concert harpists in the world. To me she looked more like a harpy than a harpist. One of her claims to fame, besides being a concert harpist, was that she had been Harpo Marx's harp teacher. I found that funny. I was a Marx brothers fan.

Shomsky invited me to an important party where he could meet contacts. Mildred Dilling was supposed to be his date, but he wanted me to tag along so we could be together. We were now tied to each other with invisible strings.

The great Mildred Dilling met us in the lobby of the Plaza in an evening dress and mink coat. She was surprised to see me on Shomsky's arm. She had invited Shomsky to this fashionable and sophisticated black-tie party to be her escort. Now I was on his arm, and Mildred the Great not only seemed annoyed but showed her jealousy. Shomsky knew that she was represented by his old impresario, Sol Hurok, who booked her all over the world at very high rates. He wanted Mildred to put in a good word with Mr. Hurok for him. And it was then that I entered the strange but slapstick world of his opportunism. Mildred was an instrument who could lead him back into greatness.

"It's all about contacts," Shomsky had said to me as we were getting dressed for the party. I had brought down from Bennington a long black satin skirt, red evening shoes, and a white blouse, and Shomsky declared that I would be the star of the party. When Shomsky complimented me, I blushed, because he kept referring to me as a woman. It was my new, sophisticated label and I loved it. I was no longer just a girl to Shomsky; I was his beautiful woman.

So this is the art world, I thought. I remembered a book I had read at Bennington with quotes from Picasso, who said,

"Art is a lie." I could see that art was created by people in the music world—as well as in every other part of the art world—who were opportunists, predators, and skilled liars. Art was a business, I was finding out. And if you didn't kiss ass and kick ass, you never got anywhere. Shomsky, with his new-found ambition to be a recognized genius, had to get back to Hurok, because without a manager you were dead. You might as well play a harmonica in an Italian bar. To be in the concert world you had to push. Push. Push. You had to rub shoulders with society. You had to have contacts. Most of all, your personality was what got you into the position of being chosen to play the fiddle in concerts. After all, there were only about ten famous concert violinists in the world—and Picasso claimed there were only ten *artists* in the world. He was talking about painters, but I was beginning to see that what was true for painters was also true for concert artists, writers, dancers, actors, poets, sculptors, architects. There was plenty of supply and not that much demand. And artists all needed patrons. So Shomsky was going to this party to sniff out patrons the way pigs sniff out truffles in the woods.

Now Mildred Dilling was looking at my womanly attractions and was clearly annoyed that her date, Shomsky, had brought along a pretty, chic, and very young woman to what she clearly thought of as her party. But Shomsky was an incredible diplomat: he kissed her hand and lied, saying that I was his niece who was visiting from her college in Vermont. So there I was, looking at my first lover, the man I was so madly in love with, and having to go along with his subterfuge. I was floating in a nightmare.

Still, I reasoned to myself quite pragmatically, *it's better than having been left behind in the hotel while he does his business socializing.* I was proud of the fact that I ignored Mildred's jealousy.

It really wasn't a party for him to enjoy himself as much as it was a party for him to promote himself and pitch "Shomsky" to everyone who could possibly help him in his career. Oh, Harpo! What a strange world.

"Miss Dilling and Mr. Shomsky," Mildred told one of the doormen as we were announced over the intercom. I felt humiliated that I wasn't one of the announced visitors, but I pretended that this oversight on Mildred's part didn't matter to me at all. *A fool vents her feelings, but a wise person holds them back,* I told myself. It was to be the first of many humiliations, but I smiled at Mildred and hid my anger.

Once in the elegant living room of the floor-through, fifteen-room apartment, I followed behind Shomsky and Mildred like an extra in a movie. They were the stars. I was a nobody.

"Who is the party for?" I whispered to Shomsky.

"Horst P. Horst, photographer of the fashionable," Shomsky said in a low voice, annoyed that I was whispering. He pointed out an elegant, white-haired man who seemed to me to be in his sixties (but who turned out to be in his fifties). "His photograph, taken in 1939, of a model wearing an unraveling Mainbocher corset and which appeared in *Vogue,* is one of the most reproduced images in the world," Mildred chimed in, as if I were some kind of dunce. But I was a dunce in this world because I'd never heard of Horst P. Horst. I read *Poetry* magazine, not *Vogue.*

As we talked quietly in a corner, a servant brought a crystal flute of champagne. I could feel myself shrinking into *Alice in Wonderland.*

"He really is the twentieth century," said a young man with a high voice who was standing next to us. "Chanel adored Horst and left him most of her furnishings. He has an exquisite eye for detail." I was surrounded by rabbits and queens, like Alice.

The room was suddenly filled with much older artists,

actors, musicians, ancient fashion editors, society people. I observed everyone swirling around Horst and watched Shomsky saunter into this sea of celebrities and rich people. Shomsky was almost like a younger, blond version of Horst himself: tall, tanned, and muscular. As Shomsky walked over to the guest of honor, people started swarming like mad rabbits around him as well. The buzz of society gossip was in the air.

"Isn't Horst divine?" a woman clutching an annoyed poodle asked me in a phony voice. "The people he knows, the clothes he photographs conjure up a world where elegance and manners still matter. I do believe that Horst P. Horst himself is a specimen of prewar savoir faire. His settings are often stylized, but what makes him Horst is his exquisite if slightly eccentric eye for detail." She gushed on. "I remember in his early days at *French Vogue* he would get rid of overly fastidious fashion editors who tried to make his settings sterile and immaculate, fussing with a stray wisp of hair or a wilted flower that was not in place. Horst wouldn't stand for that. He told me, 'My best pictures always have a little mess—a dirty ashtray or something.' Isn't that brilliant?" Oh yes, I had gone down the rabbit hole.

And I was out of my element. I was uncomfortable because I hadn't realized I would be so ignorant of all this high-life conversation. I was so much younger than everyone else there. I felt as if I were living in a foreign country with Shomsky and Mildred and social climbers who were pretentious and laughable. What kind of world was this? I felt curiouser and curiouser.

As I stood alone, Shomsky came by and swooped me out of the room. "I've said goodnight to old Mildred," he said. "Let's go home and make love. I've met who I've had to meet." I realized suddenly that Shomsky's work was being charming. If I wanted to fit into his world of society, I had to realize that even at parties, Shomsky was "working the room." He was selling himself. He was, after all, a concert performer. I was happy to leave, but still I was flattered to be included with older people who were so different from my girlfriends at Bennington.

After I graduated from Bennington and spent a few months living at the Dryden Hotel with my father, I allowed Shomsky to arrange my life so that it would be easy for us to have a lovefest of our own without my having to come home to the Dryden every night.

A certain white-haired Mrs. Barret made brassieres in a small, brown building on 57th Street between Park and Madison Avenues. Her claim to fame was that she had "invented" the wired bra. Shomsky lied to her, saying he needed a small rent-controlled apartment for himself. One had just become available in the walk-up building. She was smitten. She was another older woman whom he romanced. Soon, the obliging Mrs. Barret provided him with the requested apartment, hoping that meant he would be near her. But he fooled her, and after he signed the lease he moved me in. Later, I sublet my apartment and joined him in Greece. Poor, single, old Mrs. Barret was furious. She wept into the cups of her brassieres because she had been scammed by the man she'd hoped would be her lover.

One thing was definite. My father did not want me to marry Shomsky.

"Why not?" I demanded.

"He's a phony."

"He is not."

"He looks like a fairy to me," my father declared.

Stella Adler, the great acting teacher, who enjoyed my daddy as a confidant and held her acting-school classes in the basement of his Dryden Hotel, which she rented for a fortune, agreed with him. "Such a beautiful girl, wasting her life on someone not stable or even willing to make a commitment. She could do better, my darling Sidney," Stella told him. "Your daughter is with the wrong man. Sidney, you should stop this. Nip it in the bud before she makes a great mistake and ruins her life—and ruins yours, too."

But I listened to no one. I was in love. Shomsky sent me a one-way airline ticket so I could join him in Greece. A few weeks later we flew to Israel to be married near his father and the rest of his family. His mother was dead. I wrote to my father that I had married Shomsky in Israel and we planned to move to Paris. My father was furious and heartbroken that his only child was going to live on another continent. He had to stay in New York and run the hotels and Ace Builders Supply. I sensed his misery when he threatened to disown me. But Shomsky had no concert bookings in America. The solo recital that he had given at Carnegie Hall, paid for by Victor Borge, had been a flop. He had been nervous, and flops are not forgivable in the concert world. He insisted that we begin our married life in Paris.

And that was that. I fled the birdcage of my father's hotel like a newly freed canary. I wrote:

> My father kept me
> in the golden cage
> of his own loneliness
> of his old age.
> My feet no longer twirl around the swing.
> Marvel that I sing
> my songs into the chatter of a law,
> though I will never
> please my emperor.

"I don't want to be a musical Jesus Christ," Shomsky told me when we arrived in Paris. "The world's greatest manager, Sol Hurok, has dropped me." Shomsky said that after he'd received a few bad reviews, Hurok got cold feet and wouldn't represent him anymore in America or Europe. No Hurok, no concerts. Shomsky's agent in Paris was "about to croak," so she was unable to provide the bookings he needed. "But it doesn't matter," he said. "I know there are conductors who will help me get to be a star again, my darling, my sweet honey bun, as I was as a child. Don't worry, I'll support us and take care of you."

"What conductors?" I asked.

"All of them. Bernstein loves me. Munch adores me. René Leibowitz, who is considered brilliant by the avant-garde, has pull with many radio orchestras. Mitropoulos wants me to play with him in Athens. There's a young conductor from Hungary who has a new orchestra in Switzerland. And Jacques Bazire, husband of the dancer Colette Marchand, wants me to open the season in Cannes during the film festival. I will take care of you. You'll see. In a few years, all the conductors will be giving me work. I've heard that Zubin Mehta thinks I'm the greatest violinist in the world. Someday he will be my brother. Meanwhile, you will be my little ersatz manager. I'll give you the addresses of orchestras to write letters to, conductors, Jewish organizations. I'll give you numbers to call. We will go to every concert in Paris and afterward to the parties, and to the receptions where the world of the very rich gives you contacts and connections. It's not how you play, my sweet little wife; oh no, it's who you know. Once we find an apartment of our own in Paris, we will go everywhere and know everyone, and more concerts will come."

I was breathless and believed him because I was in denial that so far no orchestras had made any overtures to him.

Paris, 1958. Shomsky was now my career. He was now my husband. It was now my job to constantly hunt for apartments, which were always on a short-term lease. We were gypsies, moving every month to another cheap place. It was also my job to iron shirts, buy food, cook, wax floors, write letters, soothe his neck, carry his violin, answer phones, make appointments, and fan his genius with my love. Once in a while I had to make love, but that wasn't very important to Shomsky; it was much more important for him to be noticed than to be intimate. To be honest, Stella had told my father that Shomsky was bisexual. I wondered what all those good-looking young men were doing at our parties. I could be wrong that he liked to be admired and loved by these men, but making love to his wife was not a high priority. It was somewhere down the list, like shining one's shoes, or something to talk about but not actually do. I was very frustrated sexually, but since I had never been to bed with anyone else, I had no idea what I was missing. And that is the good thing about marrying a virgin. I was so happy to be in love that I didn't really know what love was, and I didn't know it had to be consensual, a two-way street. This was a street that had a dead end, and the dead end was our bed.

I was no longer Sandra but Joan of Arc, out to do battle for my musician husband. I wore the armor of my innocence and my love. When you're a woman, you embody what P. T. Barnum said about suckers. He said a sucker is born every minute, and now the sucker was me. After all, I was in the circus of marriage. I was in the freak show. I was a seal with a ball on my nose. I was an elephant with a chain on my leg. I was on the flying trapeze without a net. I was the world's biggest fool, but it would take a little time for me to realize that.

The obstacle of poverty was not what I feared. In fact, in those days I feared nothing. Making love with Shomsky at night—kissing his suntanned body, biting into his neck with playful kisses, biting his lips, holding him in my young but maternal arms—kept me agog in bed. I fell from the hell of the daytime into the mysterious crevices of the night. In the beginning I knew that I could make him happy. But it's hard to make a man happy who has no work. Every day I felt that I was melting—as if I were the Joan of Arc statue in the Place de la Concorde but made out of lard and vanishing in the sunlight. An occasional concert in Greece or Portugal or Holland or a second-rate tour kept us alive.

Winter 1960. Paris. Like a shadow, I trailed behind Shomsky in the snow. We went to a violin maker's atelier, where he lent us a little money. We were always begging or borrowing. We decided if we ate one meal a day we could save money, and we often ate in the cheapest restaurants, where we mostly ate kidneys and innards because they were the least expensive items on the menu. Shomsky found an unbelievably cheap restaurant in an old building where you walked up four flights, and there was a dining room for Catholic children, run by nuns. We could sit with the children and have our lunch, paying practically nothing. I liked being with the children. To me they were more interesting than the bourgeois adults that Shomsky knew. They laughed, they joked, they had food fights, they ran around the tables. But at least we were eating. Shomsky didn't care too much for that experience, but it was the cheapest meal you could get in Paris.

Shomsky was a genius at getting things for nothing when it involved bargaining with older women. Almost all our apartments were apartments that Shomsky conned some old woman into giving us in return for my being the apartment sitter and cleaner. That was how I learned something I have never forgotten: to wax a floor you don't have to bend down with a cloth; you can tie rags on your feet and practically dance on the floor, and it shines.

We sat at the Café Deux Magots in Paris, where Shomsky held court. He was a known figure in Paris, having lived and concertized there most of his life. And I sat by him, an innocent young American wife who had never really known what poverty was. Shomsky laughed and joked, and no one suspected we were broke. Laughter covered up our anxiety about money.

We moved, that first year in Paris, from one cheap hole-in-the-wall to another. I didn't care. I stayed up all night typing letters to managers. I became aggressive with managers, pitching Shomsky to whoever would listen. He was my husband. He was a genius, he had had a terrible life, he had escaped the Nazis, and he was still alive. One day, the legendary Igor Stravinsky, short, bald, and good-tempered, came to one of our sordid apartments. Another day it was Shostakovich, who was on a trip to Paris. He was visiting us because Shomsky had played in the Soviet Union. Both of them overlooked our poverty and were thrilled to listen to Shomsky play their music on his violin. I felt privileged to be married to such a great artist. The fact was, I was finding out the truth about being unsuccessful. You never think of art; you only think of money. Before our marriage, I had imagined that Shomsky and I would have esoteric conversations about the last period of Beethoven, or the meaning of Chopin's études. On the contrary, all we talked about was how we could not pay the rent or where I could buy the cheapest horsemeat. Who did we know that could lend us money. Poverty was as rampant as a covered-up gum disease.

Finally, my father got word from friends of his who'd visited us that we were starving, and he broke down and sent us two hundred dollars a month. But even with that money, which was hardly a fortune, without concerts we had no future. We were paupers who had to always pretend we were successful. If the concert world sniffs your poverty, you're finished. We had to keep up appearances.

*   *   *

I remember becoming weary while looking for apartments in Paris. Upstairs and downstairs. Leaks and cold water. A phone call from my father: "My daughter shouldn't be running around with a bunch of no-good artists." I didn't hear him. Instead, I put aside money for months and rented a convertible and drove to Normandy—to be myself, whoever I was. I had such anxiety about poverty that I suffered nightmares. One time, I woke up breathing through gills. I had turned into a sea maiden and set out for the dangerous place underwater. In my dream I saw my father: "You have to come home," he said to me. I stood there, drowning. Then I woke up. Dream over.

Finally, Shomsky gave a concert in the South of France and took me along with him. The first time I saw the legendary Jean Cocteau, he was wearing a black cape and a white linen suit, and in his lapel was the Légion d'Honneur. He seemed old and fragile. We were at the Majestic Hotel in Cannes. Cocteau looked like his photographs except there was a gentleness about him, almost as if he were a white unicorn caught in the web of sunlight in late afternoon, agreeably welcoming Shomsky and me. We joined him for tea. Shomsky and Cocteau began talking about the Cannes Film Festival. Shomsky had forgotten to "present" me, and immediately Cocteau asked about me and presented himself. He was so French and so polite. Shomsky told him I was a poet and bragged about my talent. Sitting in an elegant wicker chair in the sunlight of Cannes, Cocteau seemed more than interested. Here was the literary giant who had been one of the inventors of surrealism in films, had brought Dadaism and surrealism into the mainstream, and was a totally original filmmaker and a poet's hero. And I was now, for a moment, the object of his curiosity. As a young poet, disillusioned with literature and the art of cinema as he found it, Cocteau had set about completely reinventing the gestalt of filmmaking. It was said that he had been the ancient lover of the poet Raymond Radiguet, the handsome writer who had written *Count d'Orgel's Ball* and had died very young. Now, as the world knew, Cocteau was the lover of the incredibly beautiful, young, blond actor Jean Marais, who had the body of Michelangelo's *David*.

Suddenly Cocteau began speaking very rapidly to Shomsky in French, and I understood that they were talking about me, as if I weren't there. Cocteau turned to me, speaking English slowly, and spontaneously invited me to be one of his English-speaking assistants. If I liked, I could work for him in Paris, along with several others he employed—young poets gathering information, helping him with his books and projects in the cinema. "I pay very handsomely," he said in French. It was, miraculously, a door opening to me—a door to a marvelous job where I could be paid, be under the wing of a great master, and, above all, learn from him. Cocteau was known to be very generous, and this was the perfect job. The chance to work for a great poet who was in his last years and needed my youth.

"Don't be silly, she's not going to be anyone's clerk," Shomsky responded in French. He was angry and offended at the idea of my working for anyone but him.

"Why not? It's the perfect job for her. And for me it would be ideal," Cocteau said again in English, smiling at me. Cocteau looked at Shomsky. I didn't see how Shomsky had anything to lose. Cocteau was a giant, a great artist, who could even be helpful to Shomsky in his career. He was a well-known aging homosexual, so there was nothing for Shomsky to be jealous about. We certainly needed the money. His offer came out of some deep, generous part of Cocteau that was sensitive to the fact that I needed help, that Shomsky and I were poor and money was only too welcome. He also told Shomsky he found me beautiful, and beauty was the most important thing in the world to Cocteau. To me he was the inventor of beauty.

Please, God, let Shomsky say yes, I prayed silently.

"No. No. She works for me, dear friend Jean. I couldn't possibly share her." And suddenly I realized that my husband *wanted* me to be dependent and without money. I could say nothing. My life belonged to my husband. I was wearing, as my father said, "the apron of marriage."

I was heartbroken when we left the Majestic, and I knew only too well that Shomsky would never allow me to see Cocteau again. Was I Alice? Or Joan? Or Sandy, Madame Shomsky?

Reluctantly, Shomsky's Parisian friends tolerated me as his new young wife, but none of his female friends became my friends. They were often middle-aged women who resented the fact that I deprived them of Shomsky's affection and attention. Another concert artist, Miriam Solovieff, was the bitch to end all bitches. She had been a violin student with Shomsky before the war, studying under the tutelage of Maestro Bronislaw Huberman. Shomsky and Miriam had both been child prodigies, and Shomsky showed me a picture of the two of them when they were young. He confided to me that Miriam was from America, that her mother had once had a brief affair with the great and talented black actor and singer Paul Robeson, and that her father had tried to shoot her mother afterward, wounding her severely. At first, this made Miriam sound glamorous, although I wasn't sure it was true. Miriam had given concerts all over Europe. But, like Shomsky, she was broke. Often they practiced scales together in our freezing apartment. Afterward, I often served tea. Miriam treated me as if I were the maid, not Madame Shomsky. It was my job to be good in bed, cook, shut up, and write endless letters on my portable Olivetti, on which I had written so many poems at Bennington.

The first time Miriam called on Shomsky and his new wife, I could tell that she was obviously jealous of me. She was like a witch who gave me the evil eye. Shomsky was now nearly forty, and she was about his age. I was the younger intruder. She questioned me in a mocking tone, asking me what I knew about the violin, violinists, and music. I was, to her, an outsider in the private world that she and Shomsky belonged to. As two concert artists, they lived in a privileged musical cocoon of arpeggios and cadenzas. Miriam often called to invite Shomsky to dinner without me, but Shomsky insisted on taking me. I sat and listened to them dish. Miriam and he gossiped constantly about conductors—Bernstein, Munch, Furtwängler, von Karajan were all subjects of their gossip. Then they went to town on the techniques of other concert violinists. Elman? He was getting too old. Nathan Milstein? He was pampered by too much money and was getting sloppy. Kagan? Overrated. Oistrakh? His sound was not what it seemed to be on recordings. Szeryng? No real energy. Heifetz? Here they argued. Shomsky said he was a god. Miriam thought his technique was overrated. Then they got around to pianists. More ennui. Gina Bachauer? "A fat slob who without her husband would be nowhere." Sigi Weisenberg? "Good technique. Lousy timing." Katchen? "Overrated." Wanda Landowska? "Limited." Van Cliburn? "Too Hollywoodish." Horowitz? "Great, but uneven." And then acoustics of the various concert halls were discussed for hours. They were happy being bitchy together.

Many of our evenings were spent going to cafés with Miriam, who always invited only Shomsky to join her. But like the Bobbsey twins, he and I were one. Miriam turned her head away from people who might be watching and said to my face a few words that let me know how she looked down on me.

"Don't you ever dress?" she asked.

"I'm not sure what you mean, Miriam," I said.

"Come on. You know what I mean. You're Madame Shomsky. Shomsky has a place in Paris society that you should maintain. Look at your shoes."

I knew they were frayed old shoes from college.

"Your pants are worn out. Try wearing a dress, why don't you?"

Miriam the bitch always wore suits and always blabbed that her "hero" was Prokofiev. She had a space between her somewhat yellowish teeth, and tiny lines were creeping around her red lips. Her fingernails were violin-short. On one of her cheeks was the famous red "rash" that violinists always have from holding the violin between their shoulder and their cheek while they play, which is worn like a badge of honor. I was about to cry. Shomsky came back from the men's room, and Miriam smiled like a cat licking her whiskers, as if nothing were wrong. I sat, silently feeling the humiliation. I played the sacred choral music of a Byzantine chant in my head as I tried to distance myself from both of them.

Somehow, I knew that of course I didn't fit in with Shomsky's older friends. His artistic circle had been developed over a period of many years, and I was the new intruder. The young little wife. No one knew I had a brain. Or a name of my own. Or had published poetry. I was just the pretty American girl Shomsky had married and brought back to Paris. No one knew that I was the star of the Bennington literary department, that I had been chosen by Donald Hall as one of the ten best college poets in America and had been published in *New World Writing*. My poem "Silence" had encouraged me to really feel that I was a poet since I saw my name in print in a popular magazine with a stitched spine. No one knew that I had won the Silo poetry award, or that I had corresponded with Katharine Hepburn, who loved my poetry. Conrad Aiken, Richard Eberhart, Richard Wilbur, and James T. Farrell, who was my friend and mentor, also loved my poetry. I had sent poems to all of them, and they had responded with beautiful letters. Nobody knew that my teacher, Howard Nemerov, was my biggest fan and had sent my poetry to the *New World Writing* Contest without even asking me. And that when I won, he told me that I would be a great writer someday. Nobody knew that my father was a big shot in the real estate world. And that Nelson Rockefeller invited him often to his home to get his opinion on deals. I was just eye candy.

I was beginning to learn how to speak French, but I had nobody to talk to. Still, maybe Miriam was right about clothes. If I'd had money, I would have been one of the best-dressed women in Paris, because I had good taste. But all the money we had went for Shomsky's clothes, not mine. My father's allowance permitted me to buy Shomsky a scarf at Hermès so he looked successful and well-to-do. And I was still wearing what was left of my Bennington wardrobe.

When I met Shomsky at twenty, I thought of him as my god and hero. Now, three years after our "courtship," and tied to each other in marriage, the husband had replaced the lover. It was as if Shomsky had stepped into a mirror and emerged as another person. He was slowly becoming my antagonist, oblivious to my needs. He seemed no longer to respect me. He was, I was afraid to admit, a stranger. It was all about him. I had to deny what was happening.

At all Left Bank cafés sat feisty girls and handsome boys my own age who seemed carefree and laughing and young. I could tell that they were mostly students from the States or other parts of Europe who were in Paris to absorb the culture and learn French. They were always laughing and having a good time. I, on the other hand, was almost like an old woman. Although I was their age, I had so many responsibilities that I felt ancient. Delmore Schwartz wrote a poem called "Vivaldi." I carried it with me from one apartment to another. It was the object that I loved, and it was torn out of the *New Yorker*. The first line read, "First love is true love; there is no other." Was he right? I doubted my own mental ability to continue being a second banana. It was a bad vaudeville show. I wished I had my girlfriends from Bennington near me in Paris. I missed all my friends. Frankly, I missed America. I really didn't want to be an expatriate. Did people sense that my love was gone? Where did it go? Maybe it was in the folds of my coat.

After we were married, my husband never asked about my poetry again. I sat in our Paris kitchen one morning and wrote this poem to remind myself that I was still an artist, even though nobody in Paris knew it but me. I dreamed Shomsky was on a journey.

My Love after a Long Journey

My love after a long journey comes home.
Wrists of time move as they move
before.
Time pounds on the window and pounds again.
And what seems like time is only the rain.
Left without our harvest of salad and Greek vermouth we hide in the
  kitchen.
An ivory snake's tooth is in the kitchen stove and cubes of ice;
dinner is all we have left of Paradise.
Adam and Eve inside of us who died are angry shadows on the
windowpane.
I see death in the black spots of a radish.

I hid my poems in a cabinet in the bathroom, where Shomsky could not find them. He would be annoyed at the thought that I wasn't paying attention to him but was writing poems instead.

I was constantly nervous. Why? I suspected that my husband had a mistress and was betraying me behind my back with his old Israeli "friend," so he said, Miriam. I supposed it was the Parisian way of marriage. But I wasn't French; I was American.

I wouldn't stand for that, and Shomsky knew it, so he was constantly lying. Decked out in the most expensive Chanel couturier clothes, Givenchy coats, capes, and suits, Alexandre hairdos, and only the highest and most expensive heels made in Paris, Miriam was a dish. She was tall with black hair, a huge, pointy bosom, and a thin waist, and she had been one of the first Miss Israels. Her fat and vulgar Russian husband, a wealthy furrier, lived with her on the Rue Pleyel. He obviously bored her.

Miriam and Shomsky had known each other for years. They jabbered away in Hebrew so that I did not understand one word. Shomsky was all aflutter when Miriam came to visit one afternoon at 36 Rue de Lille, where we were living for free.

"Please play, Shomsky darling," she said in her broken English. Amazingly, he went, like an obedient puppy, to the bedroom and dragged out his violin. I was shocked because Shomsky never concertized at home for anyone except other violinists. This Miriam, I knew, had a special grip on him. He came back to the living room, plucked a few broken hairs out of the bow, lifted the beautiful fiddle to his chin, stretched out his neck, and raised the bow with his long, beautiful fingers. He began to play the Bach Chaconne.

It was instantly irresistible. The melody filled the room in an almost sacred way. Miriam's perfume, Joy—which I recognized—also filled the living room. It was a heavy-scented smell of leaves of roses mixed, it seemed, with her perspiration—and I could sense that Miriam, the furrier's wife, had designs on my husband.

"Shomsky, darling, you should be playing on a Stradivarius."

"Of course I should, but they cost a million dollars," he laughed.

"My husband might want to buy one as a business investment. You never know." She was outrageously trying to buy Shomsky, not a Strad. She thought she was so smart, but I was on to her.

"I would dedicate all my concerts to you, Miriam darling, if you could buy me a Strad." Shomsky walked over to her with his violin beneath his chin. "Let me play something special. The Bartók."

I felt so angry as I sat there listening. I had to put some logs on the fire until Bartók was finished. "What a sweet little wife you have, Shomsky," Miriam said before breaking back into Hebrew to tell a joke, which I didn't understand. *Fuck you,* I thought. I couldn't wait for her to leave. A few minutes later, she picked up her fox coat and fox hat and indicated that she was leaving. I hoped I would never have to see her again.

"I know you're having an affair with Miriam," I confronted Shomsky right after she left.

"Don't be silly."

"I'm tired of waiting on women who insult me."

"She didn't insult you."

"Oh, really? Why do you have secrets in Hebrew that I can't understand?"

"What secrets? We were telling jokes."

"Why don't you tell *me* a joke? I could sure use a laugh."

"You're crazy," he said.

"Is that supposed to be funny? I thought I could help your career. Let Miriam buy you a Stradivarius. Now I just want to go back to America. I want to get a job. I want to go back to writing. I want to go back to school. I'm sorry. I feel isolated, Shomsky. I need someone just to talk to. I miss my girlfriends at Bennington. I miss my daddy and Aunt Jewel."

"Don't act like a spoiled child. You don't know anything about life. Your father sent you to expensive and snooty schools. Did you ever work for a living? Have you ever sold a poem? Or a story?"

"I haven't had a chance to try. You put me to work for you. I did sell four poems while I was in New York, and one short

27

story, for your information. Now I am your slave as Mrs.——or should I say Madame——Shomsky."

"You call being Madame Shomsky work? A lot of women would love to be Mrs. Shomsky. They would love that work."

"The truth is, Shomsky darling, I want to go home. Let one of those women you talked about marry you and work for you for nothing. I quit. I'd like to go home. My daddy would be only too happy to have me back in America."

"What did you think being married to a concert violinist would be like?"

"I didn't imagine. I just loved you. Now you're playing around behind my back. You're fooling around with Miriam. I know it. Every time she comes to see you, she's dressed up like Lady Astor's pet pony."

"She's just a friend. She wants to invest in my career. She's paying for the hall when I give my recital at the Salle Pleyel."

"Why does she want to invest, as you say? I can just guess."

"I have to have patrons. We need Miriam to survive."

The conversation was over. Shomsky went into the bedroom to practice scales. *Eeeew eeeew eee eee eee eee eee,* screeched his violin.

Miriam was now a part of the Shomsky career. She had replaced me in his affections. She became a ubiquitous part of our lives. Wherever she went, she telephoned Shomsky. We often found ourselves joining her for drinks at the fancy George V Hotel or for tea at the Ritz—she sent her chauffeured Rolls-Royce to pick us up. We had lunch at the Brasserie Lipp. While journalists such as Sartre and other existentialists sat discussing the meaning of life, Miriam sat discussing the meaning of fur. She was an idiot. At least in English. I was doomed to be polite to her.

"Do you like chinchilla?" she asked me, as if she were posing some serious philosophical question about life à la Schopen-hauer or Nietzsche.

"I hate fur," I said. "I think it's a sin to kill innocent animals."

"Not even sable?"

"Not even."

She pouted. Shomsky listened to Miriam with awe in his eyes. He was under her spell again. I had the distinct feeling that he and Miriam did much more than speak Hebrew together when they were alone.

We had become a threesome. She was glue. I no longer had a husband. I had a husband plus Miriam. One night we went to *A Taste of Honey* at the Theatre National. It was in English and had originally been produced for an English theater. It was clear to me that Miriam and Shomsky were not merely friends but lovers. And that not only was my husband having an affair, he was having this liaison, as the French would say, right in front of me. I remembered some couple—Jean and Camille, a French writer and his wife—saying, "We are an old couple. You are a new couple." Their subtext was that old couples are tired of each other, but new couples are still in love. Shomsky and I weren't in love anymore.

One night Shomsky came home and confronted me.

"I'm telling you in advance, Sandra. I decided to accept an offer to tour Greece. I have two concerts in Athens, and one in Salonika."

"When did that come through?"

"I got a call yesterday when you were out shopping for food."

"Am I coming with you?"

"Of course not. Two plane tickets to Greece are too expensive."

"Why don't you ask Miriam to lend you one of her cars? We can drive there. Remember when we were in Athens before we were married? Those were happy days. I have a driver's

29

license. It's such a beautiful drive. We can take the ferry to Hydra and have a vacation together, away from the stress of our problems in Paris."

"Miriam's working on buying me a Strad. I don't want to ask her for anything else."

"Listen, Shomsky. While you're playing in Greece, I'm going to ask my father to send me a one-way ticket to New York and I'll take a vacation. I could use one."

"Don't you dare do that."

"Why not?"

"I don't want you leaving Europe. Your home is in Paris, not New York."

"Fine."

He saw that leaving me alone could be dangerous.

"As a matter of fact, you're right. You can be useful to me on the tour. All right. I'll borrow the money for your ticket from Miriam."

"You mean it?"

"Yes," he said sweetly.

"Because I don't have any friends here in Paris," I said, beginning to cry, "or anyone. All your friends are only interested in seeing you, not us. And I can't work without a *carte d'identité*."

"Work? Being my wife is your life's work. I'm a fortunate man to have you. Sometimes I forget that. I'm sorry."

"Thank you, Shomsky. I accept your apology."

I started packing his clothes and my clothes in one large suitcase, but I knew our marriage was over. I was tired of trailing behind the great Shomsky, carrying his violin case. I wanted to go back to school and get a master's degree. I dreamt sometimes of having an apartment back in New York and giving poetry readings with Allen Ginsberg and Gregory Corso at the Cafe Wha?, where so many poets were reading and the world was interested in Beat poetry. I was on the edge of Beat. My favorite place in Paris was the "Beat Hotel."

William Burroughs lived there. Allen Ginsberg lived there when he came to Paris; so did Jack Kerouac.

New York was now the capital of poetry, not Paris. The days of Rimbaud and Baudelaire were over. In New York City and San Francisco, there were five "schools" of poetry. First, the "academic" school; that was Randall Jarrell, Alastair Reid, W. H. Auden, Richard Wilbur, Howard Nemerov, and Donald Hall, among others. The next, which was much more important, was the "New York" school of poetry: Frank O'Hara, Kenneth Koch, Barbara Guest, John Ashbery. Ashbery actually lived in Paris and was a friend of mine. I once invited him to lunch when Shomsky was out of the house; I served him raw sausage. "Aren't you supposed to cook this?" he asked. I said, "I don't know." I was blushing because I really didn't know. "If I eat this, I may have food poisoning. If you could just make me an omelet, I'd appreciate it," he said in a monotone voice. I imagined the buzz in the poetry world: "Ashbery Dies of Food Poisoning in Paris." The New York poets were the most surrealistic. They all gave readings at the Danny Meyer gallery. They were very influenced by Tristan Tzara.

The next school was the Beats. The Beats had very few women included in their success because most of the Beats were homosexuals and proud of it. Only one woman was in their tent: Diane di Prima.

I took ideas from all those schools, but I refused to be blown off my feet by any of them. The poet I admired most was Pablo Neruda and, after him, Bertolt Brecht. And after them, Wallace Stevens, who didn't fit into any school; Dylan Thomas, who was a school in himself; and T. S. Eliot, whose *Waste Land* influenced me when I was in boarding school.

Robert Lowell singlehandedly created the "confessional" school with his book *Life Studies*. Anne Sexton and Sylvia Plath were his signposts, and in a way so was I. Delmore Schwartz also fell into that category.

The fifth school was the "Catholic" school: Robert Lowell was part of it, even while being the founding member of the confessional school. In the Catholic school was my best friend Howard Hart, and also Ned O'Gorman.

Perhaps the most important poetry was happening not in New York City but in San Francisco, where Lawrence Ferlinghetti had started the City Lights Bookstore, which also had a publishing house. Kenneth Rexroth, the Chilean poet Violeta Parra, and all the Beats were published by his Pocket Poets series, which consisted of small, affordable books with simple covers and exciting poetry. Other poets in the series were Gregory Corso and Allen Ginsberg. *Howl* was the most popular of the Pocket Poets books; it was read by every young aspiring musician and intellectual and revolutionary and poet in America.

Two other poets that influenced me couldn't really be placed in any school: Ezra Pound, who said, "Make it new," and Elizabeth Bishop, who was very close to Marianne Moore. The poetry in both those women was very subtle but magnificent.

Put it all together: poetry was having its most exciting moments in San Francisco and New York City, as well as on university campuses where poets were teachers, and in art galleries. The academics never came to New York, because they stayed on their college campuses, where they got big salaries. But the Beats gave readings. Some poets—like James Merrill, who had a trust fund from his father, who ran Merrill Lynch; and Wallace Stevens, who was the CEO of a large insurance company; and William Carlos Williams, who was a doctor; and Robert Graves, who lived in Spain and wrote offbeat books— were oddballs, but brilliant oddballs.

And where was I? Carrying Shomsky's violin case into third class on a train, which went no place for me and my budding career.

There were times I thought of running away to an ashram

in India, where I would never have to think about money and could just write.

I belonged to the school of enslaved wives who played second banana to the star. Gertrude Stein liked living in Paris because she found living in a place with a foreign language "very inspiring." But I was not in any way like Gertrude Stein. I didn't have a salon, I didn't have a private income, and I didn't have Alice B. Toklas to soothe my eccentricities. I was nothing but a wife. I wasn't even a mother. I didn't know who I was. To the world I lived in, I was the pretty little American wife of Shomsky. I imagined on my tombstone it would say, "Sandra Hochman, Violin Schlepper."

Like many women of my generation, before feminism, I was locked in the kitchen. I had to let myself out. I wondered why I didn't just pick up and leave, but I didn't have the money or the courage to walk away. I couldn't face breaking up. I was too frightened to move away from my familiar misery.

We stopped making love. And I wrote, by myself, in the bathroom, at night.

The second year after we got married and were plopped in Paris by our destiny, Shomsky introduced me to the famous guru of atonal music, a disciple of Schoenberg, a cult figure among musicians, René Leibowitz. I had no idea that I would end up falling in love with him. He was a magical, mysterious figure to me. He was very tall, looked to be somewhere in his eighties (although I later discovered he was only forty-seven), was balding, had black hair that was dyed by secret beauticians, wore black horn-rimmed glasses, and had a perfect, short nose with freckles. He was twenty-four years older than me. He wore elegant beige cashmere sweaters and had a soft, seductive voice. He spoke English without an accent. He also spoke perfect French and German, and of course Polish, his native language.

I say "of course" because everyone in the sixth arrondissement knew his legend. He had been born in Warsaw and escaped to Paris just at the tip of World War II. His entire family, including his beloved brother as well as his brother's wife and children, had been captured on Kristallnacht by the Nazi butchers and later incinerated by the Holocaust death ovens in Poland.

As a fugitive from the Nazis, René became a hero in the Resistance in France, switching his allegiance from a young man's anarchy to Marxism and befriending, among others, the martyr Simone Weil. He was also friends with Camus and Sartre. At that time, René was young and daring, furiously risking his life in the underground movement. Even when I first met him, he was still a close friend of Sartre. Meanwhile, he had carried the epiphanies of the composer Schoenberg to Paris. After the war, he had many worshipping students, including Pierre Boulez. Atonal music, music without conventional melodies, was in style. I hated atonal music, but I loved him. Why? Because he paid attention to me. Arthur Miller wrote in *Death of a Salesman,* "Attention must be paid." That philosophy is true for everyone (except Arthur Miller, who never paid attention to Marilyn Monroe. But he wasn't a salesman; he was an artist, and artists are special people who always have the pardon of God).

René Leibowitz had married rich Mary Jo from Chicago ten years prior to our arrival in Paris. She was an ambitious young woman who had stolen him away from her friend Ellen Adler. Ellen had been a great beauty but had no fortune to speak of. Her claim to fame was that she was the daughter of Stella Adler, who taught acting in my father's hotel basement. Mary Jo, on the other hand, was an heiress who had gone to Radcliffe, had majored in composition, had been friendly with Aaron Copland and Leonard Bernstein at Harvard, and had set her mind on marrying the prestigious René Leibowitz the moment she met him. Mary Jo wanted to belong to his world of avant-garde leisure.

I was told that meeting Leibowitz was the greatest thrill of Mary Jo's life. She had been an existentialist groupie when she first arrived in Montparnasse, staying in a magnificent *hôtel particulier* in the sixth arrondissement. It was a twelve-room floor-through apartment that she had purchased, it was rumored, for over $3 million, an unheard-of sum in those days. Mary Jo had filled the apartment with hundreds of books transported from America, recordings of modern music that were rare and desirable, French antiques, works by Picasso, Masson, Dali, Matisse, and Giacometti, sculptures by the avant-garde artist Tinguely, and a collection of Yves Klein blue-sky paintings that covered the walls of her dining room. After she and René were married, they often gave chic dinner parties, and everyone wanted an invitation to the exclusive Leibowitz salon. I could only imagine them at breakfast gossiping about us:

"I just saw Shomsky and his wife, Sandra, at the Rothschild party, and I want to give a party for them, darling. Nothing elaborate," René would say to Mary Jo.

"I thought you hated parties," I imagined Mary Jo saying.

"Of course I do. But they're looking toward a splendid career for Shomsky, and he's wildly talented. And all he needs is a few breaks. That means the right people. Did you know Sartre loves music?"

"He does? That's odd."

"In fact, his distant cousin is Albert Schweitzer. He has told me he wants to meet Shomsky. *Tout* Paris went to all the concerts that Shomsky gave before the war, when he was very young. Let's invite as many patrons of the arts as we can and of course Jean Moreau, Barault, Alain Deloin, and I'll have my students and several literary friends."

"Shall I cater from Fauchon?"

"That's too fussy. Just champagne, and let the cook come up with one of her fabulous mango chickens."

"Eloise is out of the question. She's pregnant, and I suggest we send out for the food if you plan to have more than twenty people. What is the little wife like?"

"Badly dressed and beautiful."

"Don't fall for her. Shomsky is not going to be your friend, René, if you fool around with his wife."

"How would he know?"

"Darling, you're incorrigible. Don't you run after enough of your female students to keep yourself entertained?"

"Shhhh. You sound too bourgeois."

"Dear darling René, I am a secret bourgeois. And I still adore you."

When Shomsky introduced me to René at the party that the Leibowitzes threw for him, I could feel René's eyes undressing me, but I assumed that was the way many older men behaved, particularly in Paris, where morality was unheard of.

"Your husband is a genius" were René Leibowitz's first words to me. "Do you know how my good friend Picasso defines genius? He said to me once, 'Genius is personality with a penny's worth of talent.'" And with that remark added to his name-dropping, René moved away from me, leaving me to think that I might never see him again. I was twenty-three, so I didn't give him a second thought. I was only impressed that he was a friend of Pablo Picasso.

I was wrong. René became a constant visitor to our home, wherever Shomsky and I lived. As I began to grow more and more estranged from my husband, René became a part of my life. He was many things to me: A confidant. A father figure. He was a survivor of the Holocaust and a Renaissance man. At first I felt tremendous respect for him. Then, without my full awareness, the respect became emotional dependency, and the dependency became obsessive love. We were soon meeting

36

at bistros, having lunches, and, platonically at first, holding hands. We were slowly forming a deep attachment.

I confided to René that I was in love with language and had been a poetry major at Bennington College before meeting Shomsky. I told him that I was jealous of Anne Sexton's winning a Pulitzer Prize when my poetry had been compared to hers by the poet Robert Lowell.

"And," I complained, "I still haven't had a book of poetry of my own published."

"You must never be jealous of anyone," René warned me. "It will kill your art. You should be always joyful for every other artist's success." That night, I thought about what René had said and realized that he was right about everything. I began having dreams of René Leibowitz in which he appeared in the dark night of my fantasies, where reason was turned upside down.

"I love you," he said in my dreams. In my dreams, it all made sense. In my dreams, his head was between my thighs, and he was kissing me and making me tremble.

Was it in my dreams that I first considered sleeping with René Leibowitz? Suddenly I knew that just as a bright lightbulb blows out, and you shake it next to your ear to hear the tiny sound of a burned-out wire knocking against milky glass, the light in my marriage had gone out. When I held my marriage to my ear, all I heard was the expired filament. The electricity had been removed. My marriage with its burned-out love.

Before my first affair, I sat on a bus in Paris and looked at my husband holding on to a wrist strap, wearing a bulky camel's-hair coat I had bought for him at a sale at Sulka's when some money came in from a concert. He seemed to be a perfect stranger. I was now obsessed with René Leibowitz; all my waking thoughts, as well as my night thoughts, were about him. I was sure that Shomsky had no idea that I was considering betraying him with a man over twenty-five years older than me. Shomsky was jealous of all the very young men I talked to at superficial parties and dinners. He worshipped youth. The concept that I would feel drawn to his much older friend never crossed his mind.

But I was not comfortable with the idea of an affair. I was ashamed of my secret feelings.

Shomsky and I and René and Miriam often went to the opera together. It was at the opera *Carmen* that I realized how much I loved René. As the tenor sang the toreador song, I looked at Miriam and envied her. How lucky she was to have money. I realized that I wanted to live with René, and it frightened me. After the opera, incredibly confused about my feelings, I went home with Shomsky and wanted in all honesty to tell him that we should find ways to talk to each other, touch each other, get to know each other again. I wanted to scream, "Don't you see that by ignoring me, you are losing me to another man?" I wanted to find the fire that had first ignited my love. No fire was there now. Only ash. I wept myself to sleep. He didn't even bother to ask why I was crying. He assumed I was homesick. And that I'd get over it.

I was sick of who I had been in the past. I was sick of everything in my life except my love of René. I wanted to spend the rest of my life with him. I felt guilty. Foolish. Insane. A thought-enchanted silence filled my sleep. I was aware of a new mystery: my desires to make love to this man who cared about me.

René Leibowitz, like a good teacher, took over my education. He wanted me to go twice a week to the Collège de France, which was free to observers, to sit in on lectures. The lecture René wanted me to attend was delivered in French by the philosopher Maurice Merleau-Ponty, a friend of his. He was Sartre's contemporary, and René felt that I should familiarize myself with the language of existentialism and learn the terms. Merleau-Ponty, I learned, had been born in 1908, and his most important books were *The Structure of Behavior,* published in 1942, and *The Phenomenology of Perception,* published in 1945. His special contribution was to bring philosophy to a much-needed acknowledgment of the human body. Both phenomenologists and existentialists had tended to write as if what each human being is, above all else, is not a physical person.

I sat and tried to decipher the philosophy of Merleau-Ponty in French. René gave me a list of terminology to study. I went over it every morning when I was pretending to write letters like a good little manager to get Shomsky concerts. But one word appeared over and over in my mind. René. René. René.

It came as a shock to realize that I wanted to move beyond my marriage, to be with René Leibowitz forever.

My only surge of energy came when I saw René. I began sneaking around more often, seeing him for lunch and lying to Shomsky because René was my only way out of despair. I was amazed at how easily I could lie. I became a master of deception. This was all the more amazing to me since I had always prided myself on being truthful. I had loved Shomsky's voice, and yet now René's voice was always in my head.

"There is no one but you and never will be, Sandra," Shomsky had once said, his huge blue eyes filling with tears. And now I was the liar. I was even proud of the way I slipped on the banana peel of honesty in the vaudeville of marriage. I felt giddy for the first time in years. Singing 1950s love songs and doo-wop and primping secretly in the bathroom, I would trot out into the sun, free of the depressing apartment in Montparnasse that had no sunlight.

I remember the day René and I had lunch at La Coupole. I knew Shomsky wouldn't catch us there. Breathless, I sat down next to my teacher, René. He let me order oysters. I loved oysters. I could choose anything from the menu, regardless of price. When Shomsky and I ate in a bistro, I always had to be the check-balancer and order kidneys or stew or whatever was the cheapest item. I was the "innards girl." Shomsky always had steak, "for energy," because he was "working hard" and I was not, he reasoned. Now I couldn't wait to order the best chardonnay, glistening pale yellow in its goblet, a plate of a dozen oysters, gray, slippery, surrounded by the strangled green hair of seaweed. It gave René pleasure to see me eat. He watched the oysters on my tongue, then kissed my wet oyster-brine fingers.

One afternoon, at one of our secret lunches, René said to me, "Where's the poem?" For the first time since I was a student at Bennington, someone was really interested in my poetry. I had promised to bring a poem. I took a crumpled piece of white paper out of my pocketbook. Shyly I handed it to him. He read it out loud to me.

AFTER YOU MARRY GO RIDING

And you dream of a horse.
Eyes saddle him,
You go carefully next to him
Admiring his muscle formed like your own,
Cup your legs over his body,
Ride him through bed sheets and pillows,
Blankets, walls, and the moon,
Fix toes in his stirrups, legs cupped over his belly,
Your own flesh yoked to his flanks and mind,
Try riding with the ease of loving
As you gallop past deep fields of childhood
Riding past children.

Riding past childhood and death—
Nostrils open and close
As you kick with your baby heels
Over old fields of violence,
Kicking into the sides
Of the horse whose name never matters
As you ride for your life's sake.

René said, "You're now riding from your house to La Coupole. You're riding for your life's sake. I love the poem. I like how you express running away." He had tears in his wise brown eyes. He stared at me with those eyes that I loved so much.

"When did you write this?"

"This morning."

"I love it. You're really talented, my darling. You must listen to me," he said seriously as he drank his wine. "You must write. Every day from now on. I want you to do that, not for me but for yourself."

"I will," I said.

"We mustn't cry. Talk to me, my love. What does writing mean to you? What made you a writer?"

"What made me a writer? My mother taking me to museums," I laughed. "Apple trees that I dreamed under. Songs that I learned. Girls in boarding school. Poets in college. Old people that told me about their lives. Stranger after stranger. The Hudson River. Miami palm trees. Stones in Ossining. Fears in boarding school. Geraniums. Cats. Butterflies and moths. Cobble streets on Riverside Drive. Odd children at Cherry Lawn Boarding School. The words in dictionaries. The words in the mouths of the poor and homeless who chatted with me. All these people and places and things taught me to write."

"Go on," he said.

"When did I start writing? I was writing in my crib. I was making a dream, wishing things were different. As I stood in my crib and cried and looked out at the Hudson shining its colors in the sun, I was already evoking dreams, listening to the shrieking arguments of my parents, creating new dialogues for those who came through the house. I was writing in my sleep. Which is, I think, where all writing begins. In the iris of the eye. You give yourself your own profession by simply saying, 'This is what I am.' When my parents divorced, I wrote to stay sane. To be who I was."

"Who you *must* be," he said. His words were libidinous and seductive.

I realized that I had been talking to him for almost three hours.

"Stop talking and eat your lunch," he said. I began eating, erotically aware that René desired me as who I really was.

Suddenly, I realized that Shomsky was boring to me now because he, unlike René Leibowitz, was so narcissistic and preoccupied with himself. He seemed old to me because we never had any fun. But René, who was so much older than me, seemed young. My contemporary. Why was that? I knew that because he had such an active mind, a mind curious about everything, I was excited to be with him. As I sat across from René that afternoon at La Coupole, I knew. I knew that I was in love with him. I knew. Was there any possibility we could ever leave our spouses and be together, as I now dreamed of being? As if he were reading my mind, he said something that made me freeze with excitement.

"We were meant to be together."

There was a silence. *What absurdity,* I thought. A prosperous existentialist composer somewhere in his late forties with a wealthy wife and a child and an enormous career, and a poor young American girl with a struggling concert violinist for a husband, sitting over oysters talking about being together. Fundamentally it was absurd.

"How will all this be possible?" I asked.

He took my hand. I remember him saying, "It will be, *cherie,*" in a seductive whisper.

"How?" I wanted him to deconstruct his passion and make sense.

"We will run away. Soon. We can go to Hong Kong. They have a symphony orchestra they want me to conduct. Mary Jo has flatly refused to go. She loves our life in Paris. Our daughter is in boarding school in Switzerland. But I'm burned out, darling. If I don't make a drastic change now, when? I could support us royally; I have savings in Switzerland that Mary Jo knows nothing about. We could live on the Peak."

"Is that in Hong Kong?"

"Yes. It's a mountain overlooking the city. I'll give you everything you need to be a writer—love, attention, silence. We can have a serene and perfect existence. A room of your own. An amah."

"And Mary Jo? And your daughter?"

"Mary Jo will get over it. And my daughter can come and visit us."

He had it all planned out.

"And Shomsky?" I asked.

"To hell with Shomsky. He doesn't love you. I do. All you are to him is an unimportant shadow, a slave. I'll set you free."

I thought of my father, Sidney, in New York City. I had written a letter to tell him that a wonderful teacher and conductor called René Leibowitz had taken an interest in Shomsky's career. He had mentioned this, unfortunately, to Stella Adler one day when he descended into the basement of the Dryden to collect the rent. Stella had gone almost berserk when she heard Leibowitz's name. She loathed him. After his awakening to the truth about René, and what a prick he had been to Stella's beloved daughter, my father had written to tell me he had spoken to Stella, who said I should avoid Leibowitz at any cost. If he ever knew that I was leaving my husband for René and running off to Hong Kong, my father would hardly be able to take the news. He was always hinting that I should abandon Shomsky and come back to America. If he hated Shomsky, he would detest Leibowitz, who was his age and a married man. It was unthinkable that my father might ever know.

But I was insanely in love and no longer cared about my father's approval. I wanted to stand on my chair at La Coupole and announce to all the people dining and drinking that I was soon going to be free of Shomsky. And the strange thing was that René and I hadn't even touched physically, other than holding hands. That was what made my passion for him so exciting. I adored him before I even knew his body. I heard an inner voice telling me to never go home to Shomsky.

After that lunch with René, leaving Shomsky seemed possible. That night I had another dream that I was bareback, riding a white horse to divorce-land for my life's sake, riding beyond the streets of the past, riding to the sea, to Hong Kong, riding away from my misery.

I questioned René carefully about whether he would miss his old buddies, such as Sartre. He told me that all the conversations he had with me made him feel that we were soul mates. He could always correspond with his friends. He wanted to study Mandarin and start a new life with me in a new city.

"If not now, when?" he would ask me again and again.

I still did not have the courage to tell Shomsky.

Prayer of Praise. From my eyes I draw strength. Energy. I burst into who I am: blood-filled quarry, body of a woman, filled with blue veins running wild through my arms, pouched stomach filled with seed to be a child, knees finely covered by the gong-tilt of golden hair, sensual openings to the imagination, exits and entrances to fluids of delight. On this dark night I thank you, God the magician, for making me not stone but flesh able to draw my passion from either a stone or a miracle.

*   *   *

Like most people in love, I had a need to talk about the person I was so in love with. But who could I tell my secrets to? I was an exile in a foreign country with my husband as my only family. I certainly couldn't tell Shomsky's friends. Who could I confide in? I lived in an absurd silence.

One morning I avoided my responsibilities of writing letters and being Shomsky's secretary to meet my only girlfriend in Paris, Peggy Peterson, who was American and older than me. I didn't know her very well, but we had met on a bus and seen each other from time to time. One morning when I *had* to talk to someone, we met for breakfast in a café near the American embassy, where Peggy worked.

"Peggy, I've fallen in love with René Leibowitz," I told her, the croissant sticking in my throat. "And I haven't even slept with him."

"It's good to be friends before you are lovers. Besides, he's divine," she said. She didn't harp on the fact that he was married, or that he was so much older. Peggy had lived in Paris for so many years that nothing shocked her. She told me in confidence that she had seen René talking on television and that she was struck by the fact that he was so brilliant and articulate as well as having a great sense of humor.

"He's an icon," she continued. "He is really living history. A hero of the Resistance. Almost every woman at the embassy who has met him has a crush on him. I'm not surprised. He's the classiest guy in all of Paris."

I was reassured that I wasn't mad.

"You may not have had sex, but that will change very soon, darling," Peggy said as she paid our check. Her parting words were: "Nothing is as exciting as a mystery. The chase is what European men are interested in. They like to be the hunters.

We women also like to be the hunters, but never mind, let him chase you."

"You're so smart," I said to Peggy. "Thank you for not judging me."

"To really know Paris, you have to have an affair. The *cinq à sept,* that time when everyone is having a drink with their lover before they go home. It's as sacred to the French mentality as wine and cheese."

"But I'm afraid. Shomsky could become vindictive. If he finds out and knows I'm really not interested in staying in our marriage, he will become vicious. He has that dark side to him."

"Never be afraid of anyone, Sandra," Peggy said. And with that, she left the café. I sat and smoked a strong Gauloise cigarette, putting Shomsky out of my mind and wondering when René and I would finally make love.

Opening the doors—all night I have repeated my dream-chant, keeping my fingers on your arm as you sleep—taking it away from me—you have taken it—taken it. The spell is taken away. I recover. My eyes regain power. What you have taken is this: my juice filled with salt, my moisture that is strength—my smoke-skin, my fire. It is my dream to one day be invisible. In beauty I have walked through lumberyards, through the impatient landscape of houses falling down—childhood and separation now appear to be me as pure events. Somewhere, out on the streets of our childhood ball-throwing and saying what we meant to say—men and women are destroying each other. Sleep with me. Lie down in the folds of lumber. In dreams there is nothing left but my unwillingness to grow up: I see things I have never seen before. I eat love: a brick-colored liquid in a cup without a saucer. A thick substance, odd to find in a cup. I drink life at breakfast. Someone is chanting, "No promises . . ."

*   *   *

Seeing René with his wife was the only way for me to be near him in public. He made sure that Mary Jo invited us as often as possible to dinners at their magnificent home filled with art, books, and antiques. Sometimes they had what I called "celebrity guests," such as Stravinsky or Nadia Boulanger. Other times it was other people. I knew René had invited us so he could be near me.

During the dinners where we "ran into each other," I began to think of how relieving it would be not to have to pretend. To be having our own dinners alone when we were married.

"Is something wrong, Sandra?" Shomsky asked me one night as we were walking home in the snow from dinner at the Leibowitzes' to save money on a taxi.

Is something wrong? You fool, I'm in love with René, I wanted to scream. "Nothing's wrong." I wanted to run away as soon as possible. I'd never wanted to have a child with Shomsky, even when I'd thought I was madly in love with him. *He* was the child. How could I take care of two demanding children? Shomsky needed constant attention. He needed me all the time. But with René, I immediately began to think of having his baby. He was a man who could handle all things. I was always daydreaming of our flight.

Crystal-growing. I hear the sound. It is mostly the sound of the sea whining and weeping and suddenly letting out its great earthless roar. It is deafening. I cannot get it out of my ears, my nostrils, my belly, my long hair. It is as clear as crystals growing in a jar. It is the sound of dandelions going to seed and blowing in the wind like huge great shadows that must disappear.

*   *   *

Shomsky was in Belgium for a radio concert that René had arranged for him. It paid well, and Shomsky was to be gone for three days. The first night after he left, I went to sleep early, as I had been up early helping him pack, writing letters, and, as usual, driving him to the airport. A knock on the door frightened me. I jumped out of bed. It was eleven o'clock.

"Who is it?"

"René."

I ran in my bathrobe to the door and let René in.

I was totally ready to make love with him. He kissed me for a long time. "Let's make love later. I don't want our first time to be in Shomsky's bed. I've reserved a beautiful suite, and I've planned the entire night. Get dressed, darling. I'm taking you out."

"Now?"

"My friend the pianist Art Simmons is playing at a jazz club. The Harmony. Miles Davis is a regular. Ever been there?"

"No."

"Come on. Get dressed, sweetheart."

I climbed the steps of the duplex loft we were living in on Boulevard Raspail, where I was a fancy house sitter for some rich American painters. I took out of the drawer my black stockings and purple pants and bra that I saved for special occasions. René had only taken me to lunch or picked me up at the Collège de France or talked to me at dinner parties in his own home. I was thrilled. This was our first "date." I had never really dated anyone except a few moronic college boys, and then Shomsky. I wore black, strappy high heels, glanced in the mirror, and thought that in my black sweater and skirt I looked like an existentialist. That was the Left Bank look I wanted.

"You're beautiful," René said quietly as I clack-clacked down the stairs. I was shaking a little bit because I was so excited. "Don't worry about anyone seeing us. This place is cool."

48

The Montparnasse jazz club was dark and smoky and off the beaten track. René was a regular, and a lot of people sitting at tables drinking and smoking greeted him warmly. He took me up to meet Art Simmons. René spoke with audacity, as if he wasn't cheating on his wife at all but we were already a couple.

"This is Sandra," he said. "She's the new love of my life. We're going to be married," he said in a whisper to Art.

Art smiled. "That's beautiful, man." And his dark brown eyes showed no surprise as he continued playing the piano. I watched his black fingers grasshopper on the keys.

Oh my God, René's in love with me. And I'm in love with him, I thought as I listened to the swing music. After the next set, we left and grabbed a cab. "The Crillon," René said. It was one of the most luxurious hotels in Paris. As we sat in the cab, we embraced and kissed passionately.

The hotel lobby was so elegant. Elegance wasn't part of my hand-to-mouth life. René checked us in as Mr. and Mrs. Leibowitz. Nobody seemed to notice my shaking hands. A uniformed bellman led us to our room. The door opened. There was a bottle of champagne in a sterling silver bucket. René had planned everything. There were flowers and a silver tray with caviar sandwiches.

René began to undress. All I could do was sit on a velvet couch and drink my champagne. I had never taken my clothes off in front of any man but my husband. I was nervous, but I felt as if the bubbles were giving me courage. Slowly I peeled off my sweater, skirt, stockings, and finally my underwear until I was naked and standing as still as a crane. René stared at me with love.

"You're more beautiful than I imagined you to be." I was surprised that René's body was strong and muscular. He led me gently to the bed. Soon we were making love passionately. I felt a new kind of ecstasy. René was a master lover. I was, for the first time, in the arms of a man who was trying to think of my pleasure before his own. He made me feel comfortable, and all my nervousness was gone.

He had booked our room for two days. I didn't have to rush off, and neither did he. Mary Jo was visiting friends in Switzerland, so we had hours and hours to get used to our new condition. Lovers. I felt no guilt. Only happiness. We could sleep together the whole night.

Before we went to sleep, René talked seriously to me. "I want to tell you some words of wisdom that will help you give up your life with Shomsky."

"I'm listening," I said. Was it really me talking? Was it a dream?

"I have to tell you something important," René said. "You may wonder how I survived Auschwitz. How I managed to live through the Resistance."

"I admire you," I said meekly.

"The answer is: I determined to be a warrior. The warrior of the light knows the importance of ambition. The warrior has integrity, flexibility, elegance, enthusiasm, humility, curiosity. All the things you have."

"I'm not a warrior," I said.

"Yes, you are. Sandra, you are so much younger than me. When I am with you, your youth energizes me. And it depresses me at the same time. I will always be so much older than you. Do you really want to leave your husband and the life you have been accustomed to? Can you really be a warrior and leave everything behind?"

"Yes," I said.

"I'm ready," he said. "I've been ready for a long time."

Two days later, when Shomsky arrived home, I was sleeping. I woke and greeted him coldly. My insides were in knots. I had to be the warrior. René was making plans for us to run away together in a few weeks. A new life would soon be mine. My hostage days would be over.

I no longer would have to be the *femme de ménage* in Montparnasse in a duplex loft that we lived in for free. Shomsky went upstairs to our bathroom. It hadn't occurred to me when I put in my diaphragm, which I was still wearing, that Shomsky might look for it. I had left the round case for the diaphragm on the sink.

I heard Shomsky scream at me from the bathroom. "Why isn't your diaphragm in its plastic case?!" Suddenly I realized there was no point in lying.

"I'm wearing it," I said. "I've been making love with René. He loves me. We are each leaving our homes and running away to Hong Kong." He came running down the stairs.

"I also found this disgusting poem, which you wrote in the bathroom behind my back, about this man who betrayed me, my best friend making love to you in my own home."

I remembered the poem and knew that I had been found out. The poem went through my mind.

RENÉ LEIBOWITZ

Lonely on Boulevard Raspail.
Our bathroom was peeling to light pink.
Brushes and combs missing teeth on
The bathshelves. A box of French detergent,
Waiting to transform me.

Pictures torn out of French Vogue magazine
Shiny and pasted on the mirror
The mad women of de Kooning's latest period
published in the magazine.
Staring down. They didn't like being placed
Over the sink where no-one knew who they were.

I looked like one of them: Pouting, angry, hair always messed,
Spending afternoons inside the tub
Whenever my husband took off for more than a week
On a concert tour somewhere in Lisbon or Brussels.
I was desperate for love.

I soaked in Paris. Scrubbing the loneliness
Off my skin. Frightened. I missed him
And needed the bubble baths to keep me from crying.
I sang in the daily bath. And thought sometimes of drowning.

Tub thoughts: When I was about fifteen
Some girls held a contest in boarding school to decide
The pleasantest way of suicide. A history major,
I quoted the Romans: "Bleeding in the tub. Preferably
With slits in the wrists. And loads of rose petals."
Tub thoughts: Paris
It comes back—
My white tub filled with French detergent Fab
Which made the bubbles in the tub go high
As the Eiffel Tower when I cried.

Now who was it
I felt like drowning—Was it myself? My husband?
Or de Kooning's
American witches—screwed up and frustrated inside his mind—
Now hanging paper dolls over the tub.
American wenches looked into my world
Where they peered at my eyebrows, earlobes, feet,
with all the shrewdness that would make them great.
Scrubbed, tubbed
Before they went to bed at night like children,
Washed, dressed, helped into pajamas,
Tucked into nightmares with drowsy faces,

Saying their sexual prayers.
The painted women. And they all were me.

I became aware of needing my lover
One afternoon as I lay in the tub,
And stared at my sexual curls and at my knees. As I looked at my toes
Planted near rusty fixtures
I began singing my own opera In defense of Love
I stole a few tunes from Wagner.
I then called my lover. The atonal music teacher, René Leibowitz,
    friend of Jean-Paul Sartre.
I jumped out of the tub
Rang him up on the phone
And finding him at home
Where he happened to be writing the History of the Opera
I said, "All the pleasures of the opera
Are awaiting you."
He entered elegantly.
(His dyed hair encased in pomade—the shiny strands greased
    black over grey)
His real age falsified on his French passport.
To improvise: He joined me
In the tub—where I awaited him
Under the detergent.
How easy How easy
The electrical field of water and soap
The short distance field
Exposing us to
Washcloth and Soap—

Somehow I want to say, get it "across" to you, how moving that bath
Was—the two of us sitting in my tub. Our delicate union.
Those bursting clouds of bubbles breaking in our mouths.
And ice-water changes

Our two bodies soaked in a sea of detergent—
Dangerous arias:
"There are no limitations to our system"
He cloaked me in a terry cloth towel
And lifted me from the marble of the bath.
We turned, and waved goodbye to our sex in the bathtub.
De Kooning's angry women watch us back out of that bathroom as
We slip from their extraordinary reach.

"Don't be funny," Shomsky said. "Why are you wearing your diaphragm?" He had ignored what I said.

"I'm leaving Paris with René."

"I don't believe you."

"I love René. And he loves me. It's true."

"But he's an old man. What could you possibly see in him?" Shomsky laughed because he didn't believe me.

"We love each other and we're running away."

"Sandra, tell me you're making all this up. I don't appreciate this joke. I'm exhausted. The concert went well, but I'm tired."

He came over to the bed. Suddenly he became furious.

"It's not true. I'm calling René this minute."

He ran downstairs and picked up the phone. He nervously dialed René's number, which he of course knew by heart. Shomsky sputtered into the phone what I had told him. There was a silence.

"He's coming over."

We sat in silence. About fifteen minutes later, René arrived. Ding-dong, he rang the bell. Here comes my wonderful life, my great future. René was wearing a hat and coat as if dressed for a party.

It was to be my funeral.

"René. My wife told me you're having an affair. You're running off together."

René laughed. "Your wife is mad. I don't know what she's talking about. Really, Shomsky, she's crazy. All the time you were gone, I was home with my family working on a new book. You just woke me up. But Mary Jo can vouch for me. I would never betray you, Shomsky; you're my brother."

"You see? He denies it!"

"Your wife is totally insane," René said. "She belongs in a mental hospital. Take her to the American hospital: they have a psychiatric ward."

The moments of silence were long. I was stunned. René left. He had betrayed me. He was protecting his marriage. He was staying with the money. I was duped and shocked. I had been used. I hated him.

That was the first time in my life that I realized what evil was. Shomsky and I fought all night. Verbal arguments like Bartók cantatas from a violin.

The next day, my father happily wired the money for a one-way ticket to New York. I packed my suitcases, and two days later I was on the plane for America.

How could a man who had helped victims escape from the Holocaust betray me? He was as satanic as any Nazi. Everything he'd told me was a lie.

In the end, though, Shomsky had believed me anyway.

I had no idea what misery was until I arrived back in the States. Taking a cab to my father's hotel, I was confronted by my beloved daddy, who wasn't able to absorb all the dirt Shomsky had spilled to him over the phone. Shomsky had told him about René Leibowitz, and my father had run straight to Stella Adler to share his shock about my liaison. Stella was a grande dame if there ever was one. Tall and blond, she was the great beauty of the Yiddish theater. Her father had been the great Jacob Adler, and she had joined the group theater, been a favorite of Stanislavski many years before, and was now married to the brilliant director and critic Harold Clurman. Because Marlon Brando was her student, she was considered one of the finest acting teachers in the world. She saw my father every day since her studio was in the basement of his hotel. They were bosom pals. She was always a drama queen and a gossip.

When my father told her everything about me, and when she heard that I was in love with Leibowitz, the maniac who had dumped her daughter for a rich woman, she was able to pour the poison of hatred into my father's mind.

"He's disgusting. A pervert and practically a pedophile, Sidney dear," Stella said. "How old is she? Twenty-three? And he's *how* much older than she is? He probably heard you owned a few hotels."

My father believed Shomsky's story. The next day, I showed up in America and demanded to talk to my father. "She's crazy," I told him. "Stella doesn't know the truth of my loneliness."

"I thought with Shomsky you would be happy," he said. "You're worse than ever. How could you betray Shomsky with his own best friend?"

I listened. It was then that I began writing poetry that was from the deepest part of me. I loved my father, but he didn't understand. In my father's hotel I stayed in my room and began to change from a schoolgirl and wife into a writer. I wanted to keep writing to cauterize the pain, the anger, the sadness that followed the betrayal by Leibowitz.

I registered at the New School to take classes in literature. I wanted to wipe from the blackboard of memory my first husband, and René, and my first betrayals.

I was unable to stuff down my anger, to contain it so I could go on. But as I sat as a schoolgirl again, my veins were filled with ice-cold anger. After I arrived in the States, a friend who knew René told me that he and Mary Jo had an arrangement whereby he seduced younger women and told her every- thing and confessed. They had a marriage titillated by mutual confessions. I poured into the vessel of poems the wine, my heartbreak.

Still, I missed Paris with all my heart. The cathedrals, the patisseries, the pink light of dusk, the cafés. The vines of my heady wine of womanhood. I knew I couldn't go back to Shomsky as I lay in bed in my father's apartment. The nightmare of my childhood was a shadow that played in my head. And yet I loved my father. I knew I loved him with all my heart.

I remember I danced at the Copacabana. I see myself as a young girl dancing on the arm of my father. I hear the rolling drums under the hands of the bored drummer. I hear forks and knives scraping against the plates, hear the sounds the Mafia men and the garbagemen make as they bang their spoons, hear the jokes come over the microphone. I am going upstairs to a strange room to see Frankie Laine. I am "introduced" to him by a friend of my father. I am given a glossy face shot of Frankie Laine. He signs it, saying, "Thank you." I take the photo back to boarding school. I wonder, "Thanks for what?" He sings "Mule Train," using his whip in my head. I am shy. I am frightened of everything, even mules. I am dancing on the arm of my father. At the Stork Club. At the blue, starry Copacabana. In my wandering years, wondering what was the matter. Something inside me was wrong. I had no idea that my strangeness, my wilderness lonely, my not being anyone at all, my fear I did not exist, my fear that no one would keep me for long—was only the fact that I looked too much like father.

My father had lost his daughter to Bennington, "some crazy college" that taught her all about people he had never heard of. I remember once when I read to him, in his tasteless penthouse, from beloved writings by some of the brilliant new writers I had been exposed to, he got very angry at me.

He said, "It's all bullshit you're learning. Don't you see that you have to go into this world and make money? And money makes more money? Forget writing."

My father's girlfriend, whom I called Aunt Jewel (and whom I adored), took my side. She hated to see us fight.

"Don't you know what Emma Goldman said?" I asked. "'I'd rather have roses on my table than diamonds on my neck.'"

"I don't know who this Emma is, but what Emma doesn't know is that even roses cost money." We were sitting in the grotesque living room of the penthouse. I was scribbling.

"What are you writing?" my father asked. He was annoyed when I didn't give him my complete attention.

"Lyrics."

"What are lyrics?"

"Poems for songs." I was writing a song after reading *On the Origin of Species,* making up the music in my head.

"You're writing songs about the book about us all coming from fish?" he said, disgusted with me.

"Gefilte fish?" threw in Aunt Jewel. She adored my father and, as a gentile, was studying everything Jewish. Whenever she could throw in a word or two that showed she wasn't just a bimbo shiksa, she did. We were all suddenly laughing.

"I'll make up my own words for the song," my father said, "and I'll dance to the song." He ran into his bedroom and took out his Fred Astaire outfit: a top hat and a cane. He completed the outfit by wearing socks and his drawers. In a singsong voice, he sang a made-up song, vaudeville style:

> *The female fishy fishy*
> *Is looking for her mate*
> *His fins conceal the mating gland—*
> *They have to copulate.*

He was so *proud* of himself dancing and making up zaney songs. And now I was leaving him again.

2.

Sidney

Being the daughter of Sidney Hochman, who owned two hotels in New York City—one overlooking Gramercy Park—and the largest building-supply company in America, had its disadvantages. One of them was that my father, who tried his best to push me into the world of rich people, whom I couldn't stand, had no idea that selling bricks was not what I was put on Earth for. Poetry was my calling; art was what I cared about. How could he understand this when he had never been educated, and I had been exposed to the arts since the age of two, thanks to my beautiful mother, Mae? Daddy and I were light years apart, not just in generations but in our dreams of glory. He had fulfilled his dreams, but my dreams were very different. He didn't understand why I didn't care at all about money. But that's because, thanks to him, I had never been poor.

Shomsky represented a way out of my father's world, a world that wasn't cultured. I wanted to be a Renaissance woman. Shomsky was the Pied Piper leading me into the world of celebrity and artistic genius that I had only read about. I met his mentor, Jascha Heifetz, who invited me to his home in California when he played chamber music with Shomsky. With Shomsky I had gone several times to the stunning duplex apartment of Isaac and Vera Stern in the Beresford building, to listen to trios of Eugene Istomin, Isaac Stern, and Leonard Rose. There was a glamorous world of classical music performed by great musicians that I had never been part of. And now, by some miracle, Shomsky would lead me into this world because all his friends seemed to be famous artists. I was in awe of the fact that, besides concert musicians, he knew people like Marcel Marceau and Jean Cocteau and Jean-Louis Barrault and Melina Mercouri and the *nouvelle cinéma* director Roger Vadim. Mimes and European show-business people impressed me, not real estate tycoons.

"You're not going to stay with that meshugenah!" my father bellowed. He began crying. Sidney was a very emotional person. Tears were running down his chubby face, his large blue eyes were filled with water, his flat Russian-Jewish nose was quivering. I felt tremendous compassion for him.

He had been born into nothing on the Lower East Side, St. Marks Place. He had three brothers, one of whom died as a child by falling off the tenement balcony during a hot summer day. My father's brother Joe ran away from home and married Tess. After that marriage didn't work out, he married Aunt Marie, who helped him establish a lumber business in Philadelphia. Uncle Joe was a loudmouth boor who rarely spoke and whom my mother couldn't stand. He slept with a gun next to his bed. But I adored him because he had given me a gold heart bracelet with a stretch band when I was seven. After my parents' divorce, loudmouthed Uncle Joe and Aunt Marie wanted to adopt me because my mother was planning to ship me off to boarding school, but my father and mother agreed for once that the adoption was not to happen.

I also loved my father's other surviving brother, Uncle Henry, because he had a husky, emotional voice and because he was the only person whom my mother's parents, the Schumers, would allow to pick me up on visiting days when I lived with them on West End Avenue. Uncle Henry and my father never liked each other, but they stuck together when it came to my mother after the divorce. Our two families were like the Jewish Capulets and Montagues.

Before the War, Sidney became wealthy, taking the money his mother had saved over the years—twenty-five thousand dollars—and opening Ace Builders Supply. He always complained that he had worked "like a dog" his whole life and had suffered the humiliation of my mother's leaving him and taking me with her against his will. Unwillingly, he had spent years investing money in fancy New England boarding schools and on a fancy college my mother insisted I attend, hoping that, after all that needless erudition, I would one day live with him.

And then, like a slap in the face, I had grown up, fallen in love with Shomsky, and planned to take off to live in Paris. My father was devastated. According to him, I was leaving him alone, to die like a dog in his old age. Woof woof. Growl growl. But now that I was separated from Shomsky and had returned to my father's eight-thousand-square-foot penthouse on top of the Dryden Hotel, there was hope. Hope that his beloved, beautiful, supereducated daughter, who knew all the things that he didn't know—his daughter with the elegant table manners, who believed in Darwin as well as God, the daughter for whom he had once bought magnificent clothes and fur coats, who had one day left the clothes and coats hanging in the closet and had left him—would now stay home.

And whom had I left Sidney for? A fiddler with no money? A fairy who schlepped around the world third-class, with Sidney's daughter reduced to a servant carrying his violin? His fancy daughter hated his "off-color" jokes and was now hanging around with hoi polloi and a bunch of snooty European celebrities, many of whom weren't even Jewish. This was his thanks? I could hear all this running like a mantra through his mind as he yelled at me out of love and frustration.

"I'm in the concentration camp of old age! Help me! Don't leave me!" he cried. He was always dramatic.

"I can't help you, Daddy," I said. "I have a life of my own."

"That's a life?" The words *of my own* stung him. He believed he had created me. I had come from his sperm, his genes, his loins. I had been part of him, and now I wanted to go away again? Why couldn't I just love him and be his? Belong to him? And do as he wanted me to do? Was that so difficult? Why was I so selfish? So mean? How could I just dump him for poverty and a loser like Shomsky?

He was bitter. Angry. Imploring. Whimpering. I too wanted to cry. Cry because I sensed his loneliness. His misery. His disappointment. He had once dreamed of being the patriarch of a loving family, living a Biblical life in which he was King Solomon. Instead, his ex-wife lived in Scarsdale with her own big Biblical family while he had no one—only his gentile girlfriend, Jewel, whom he didn't love at all.

But what about me? Couldn't I bring him even a *tiny* bit of happiness? Stay and live with him? Why not? Didn't he deserve some love? Some consideration for all his sacrifice?

Sidney had a big night coming up, and he wanted me to be there. So he hatched a plan. He would somehow maneuver to make me meet another man, someone who could be a son to him, someone he could show off to his friends and introduce with pride using those magic words: "My son-in-law the lawyer" or "My son-in-law the hotel manager." He refused to be the old St. Bernard Sidney with a keg of misery around his neck. No. It was a dog-eat-dog world, and his daughter wasn't a dog. He would find her a protector, someone who would love her and support her and treat her like the princess she was meant to be. The plan began to form in his mind. It kept him alive. It was an obsession, a reason for him to live.

After I had left Shomsky in Paris and had returned to New York to live with my father at the Dryden, the building-material business association planned to honor my father at a special event at the Waldorf Astoria. In the early 1960s, the very name "Waldorf Astoria" made plump, golden sunbeams dance in the minds of the overtly ambitious. If you came from the Lower East Side, as Sidney did, the Waldorf was the antithesis of your neighborhood of origin, with its barrels of garlicky pickles and of herring floating in brine, its chopped liver with *schmaltz,* its ancient, wrinkled, red-nosed waiters with dirty shirts and hands that shook as they held thick porcelain bowls of red borscht.

The Waldorf was the place of white starched napkins and class. Or so it seemed to Sidney. A glossy souvenir book was printed in which everyone for whom Sidney had ever done a favor took out an ad saying "Congratulations" in scroll. Everyone who did business with my father or had ever used an Ace brick bought an ad. It was an expensive way of ass-kissing my father and making sure business would continue in the coming years. "To the leader in the industry. We admire your integrity," said the ad taken out by Atlas Cement, a competitor. Old man Trump, old man Zekendorf, old man Levitt, old man LeFrak—they all bought ads because my father supplied the flue pipe and cement that were in all their buildings. His glass brick had been used in the United Nations building. A distinguished description of my father's business accomplishments was listed at the beginning of the souvenir program, with a picture of him taken by Karsh that was airbrushed and made him look forty pounds thinner and ten years younger. In the portrait, he looked like Clark Gable without a moustache. There was a huge article about him in the *New York Times.*

Since God himself wasn't available as the guest speaker, the planning committee had invited the politician Averell Harriman, New York's classiest gentile. This was the highlight of my father's life.

With the emotions of a child, Sidney looked forward to the evening. His brother Joe wasn't invited because he had the reputation of getting drunk and spouting off insulting inanities to everyone around him. Uncle Henry, who was my father's business partner, had to be invited, of course. Uncle Henry, who was always a generous man ("On my money, he's generous," my father would lament. "He's nothing but a pain in the ass, and I wish I had never promised my mother I would take him in as a partner. Nobody can stand him.") took out a two-page congratulatory spread in the program.

Aunt Jewel was thrilled that she'd been invited. He usually left her out of business events because they were not married and my father's friends were a conventional crowd. But this was to be his big night, and he shopped for both of them for the occasion. Aunt Jewel got the inevitable mink stole from Sol Vogel, a Seventh Avenue furrier—wholesale, of course (Sidney was too cheap to spring for a coat). My father justified never lavishing money on poor Aunt Jewel with the convenient saying "You give them shoes, they walk out on you."

Aunt Jewel was so dazzled by Sidney's charismatic personality (which my mother had found not charismatic but obnoxious) that whatever he did she considered "sweet." He had told her a million times he didn't love her, that he would never marry her, and that he was planning, when he died, to leave all his money to me, not to someone who wasn't his life partner. But instead of that making her hate him, she simply accepted whatever he said or did with a kind smile that showed how grateful she was to even know him. Aunt Jewel was an angel without a halo.

Her own history was as tragic as that of a Dickens character. She had been found on the doorstep of a Catholic orphanage and been adopted by a very mean Catholic nurse who had given her away to an Amish couple. When the Amish couple was killed by an automobile that collided with their horse and buggy, Aunt Jewel, now a young woman, had returned to live with the mean nurse.

At fifteen, Aunt Jewel worked at a fancy fruit-and-candy store called Hicks, where she met an old man with whom she "kept company." He was from the Bamberger family of Austria, who were related to the Rothschilds. He took her home one winter to meet his mother, the family matriarch, who he was sure would disapprove of Jewel since she came from a gentile family. His family was dead set against intermarriage. To his surprise, old Mrs. Bamberger fell in love with Jewel, and the couple were married in Austria.

Aunt Jewel always loved to tell the story of how she had been chosen to sneak the Bamberger and Rothschild jewels out of Austria after the Nazi takeover by having them sewn into her girdle. On the train, the Nazis had bypassed her and her husband, calling them "American tourists." Her husband had allowed her to keep two beautiful diamond rings, which she had insisted I have as a present. She met my father when I was about twelve by being introduced to him by his manicurist. As a girl I used to ask her, "Aunt Jewel, why didn't you stay with your rich husband?"

She always gave the same reply: "Because he was so boring. And there is nothing worse than a bore." She would tell me the story of their separation over and over: how she had taken nothing from him and just walked out one day, went to work selling scarves at Saks Fifth Avenue, and never saw Mr. Bamberger again.

Aunt Jewel went on vacations with my father and me. She was so kind to me and always cooked my favorite food: squash with cinnamon and butter, and scallops with cream sauce. I asked my father *why* couldn't he marry Aunt Jewel? "*Zi shtill,*" he answered—Yiddish for "Be quiet" or "Shut up." He called her cooking "gentile food" and tried to teach her unsuccessfully how to make his favorite fatty brisket. But Aunt Jewel wasn't a brisket kind of cook. It hurt and angered me that the excuse my father used for not marrying her was that she was a gentile, since of course at Bennington most of my good friends were gentile society girls. Sidney's anti-Semitism in reverse bothered me, but his reasoning was just an excuse.

In fact, my father's closest friend was a charming old Irish gentleman named Howard Kinney, who was one of the few people my father confided in and asked over to dinner, and *he* was a gentile. "I'm not so Irish as I'm cabbage-looking, you know," Sidney would always say to Mr. Kinney, and for some reason they both would laugh.

My father always treated Aunt Jewel with a certain distant respect and called her "his attendant," even though they slept in the same bedroom. She did everything for him, including drive his car and even help him put on his socks in the morning. Now Aunt Jewel was as excited about the Waldorf dinner as Sidney was, and she made sure for the occasion that he had a new suit, new shoes, and for some reason or other a Panama hat. It was summer, and it was important to her that Sidney look well-dressed for his big night.

The night of the dinner, we arrived at the Waldorf in a limousine. Aunt Jewel and I were seated at a table, while my father was placed on the dais next to Averell Harriman. Everyone knew that Harriman collected art, and Aunt Jewel and I had coached Sidney on the names of the Impressionist painters. Aunt Jewel had even recently persuaded my father to buy two Renoirs and an Utrillo at an auction at the Park Benet as "investments"—and, of course, for prestige.

It was sad how much my father craved prestige. His "humble background" had always been an embarrassment to him because many of his acquaintances, who were second-generation Jewish immigrants, had gone to college. And yet my father loved dirty jokes and to brag about "the college of hard knocks," where he had won his diploma in "survival." He was an odd confusion of insecurity and bravado. He said whatever he felt, whenever he felt like it. "It's important to be yourself" was his motto, and it was pathetic how this evening of prestige was a validation of my daddy's identity as odd man out in the brick business, which was all Irish. He even had the pleasure of having Mr. Kelly, the father of Grace Kelly, "the movie star" (as if people didn't know who she was), sitting near him on the dais.

The real reason I was there, according to Sidney, was to see if I could meet an alternative husband to Shomsky. "Take off your fucking wedding band for the dinner. The sons of many of my friends will be there. Nobody knows you're Mrs. Shomsky, thank God, and I want you to look single. It wouldn't kill you to please me for once in your life, after everything I've done for you."

I had realized that his whole life was centered on his daughter (me). He said, over and over again until it made me insane, "You're all I have." To let my father have his one evening of happiness, I decided to give him a little *knokis* and pretend that I was "eligible." I had eloped with Shomsky in Israel, and my father had never had the chance to show me off to his world at a wedding.

Shomsky had been calling me from Paris every morning and begging me to come back to him, saying the "Leibowitz disaster" was a thing of the past and we should start "fresh."

I received telegrams from Vienna, where he was staying at the Palace Hotel and playing the Bartók violin concerto for some fancy charity. There were plans for a royal ball, where kings and queens and other weird Disney-like people with real crowns were going to be dancing in a castle, and he begged me to show up. But I had refused and instead decided to go to the building-material ball with my father and give him the happiness he had wanted all his life—happiness that was so elusive to him because it all meant nothing. "If you're not there, how can I be happy without you?" he asked, throwing in his inevitable Sidneyism: "You'll see one day when you have your own children."

I knew his Sidneyisms by heart. The most recent one was "Fine birds need fine feathers," and he had spent a fortune dressing me for this occasion. Aunt Jewel had taken me to Bergdorf Goodman and bought me a beaded white gown (I hated beads, but my father insisted that Aunt Jewel get me a dress that looked glitzy, not gentile). As I tried on my two-hundred-dollar Cinderella slippers, all I could think of was how I was used to running around Paris in my old black velvet pants that had a urine smell in the crotch because we could rarely afford a dry cleaner. And how I usually wore my Bennington sneakers or old boots that had been to the French shoemaker at least ten times to mend the heels or the sole or the tips. I had even been treated by my father to a day at Kenneth's Beauty Salon, where I had my hair streaked and piled on top of my head with a string of rhinestones woven in.

"Nothing's too good for my princess," my father would say. I enjoyed being spoiled and pampered, even if I knew it wasn't going to last very long. I knew that my father was a tormented but funny and good person in his own way, and I wanted to give him the illusion, at least for a few days, that I was the kind of "solid citizen"—translate to "bourgeois daughter"—that he really wanted me to be.

He had been cursed by having as a daughter a wild-woman poet instead of a good Jewish woman who marries a rich man or goes to law school and becomes a judge or lawyer. A pillar of society. "Did I work my whole life to have a misfit? An outsider?" he asked. Although he had never heard of Kierkegaard or Sartre, he wasn't interested in *my* existential questions. For him there had never been such a luxury as "finding yourself." It had been work like an animal or die. He hadn't had the luxury of going to college to study "the meaning of meaning" with Howard Nemerov, or "language of symbolic action" with Kenneth Burke, or *The Tangled Bank: Darwin, Marx, Frazer, and Freud as Imaginative Writers* with Stanley Edgar Hyman. He had managed to meet a smart, well-educated, and stunning woman, my mother, and copulate with her in Cuba—and out had popped me. I had gone from the adored little daughter to the brat my mother and her second husband wanted nothing to do with, and I had not so much grown up but morphed somehow into an overly gifted child at Cherry Lawn School. My education made me as distant from my unschooled father as, say, a person from Jupiter was from an Earthling.

That education had put a chasm between us. My father had never really read a book. Sometimes he claimed he had been bar mitzvahed, but even that wasn't true, and he never read Hebrew or English. Because of his salesman's personality, which he had cultivated out of necessity, he had entered the basically all-Irish world of the building-material business at thirteen, and had learned, while still at Anderson's Brickyard, how to woo, schmooze, flatter, and cope with a strange world. He had always taken the "boys" out to bars and had bought drinks for his customers. He had knelt at St. Patrick's Cathedral with some of his biggest customers, had gone to wakes, had no qualms about drinking Irish whiskey and singing Irish songs. He told dirty jokes or even anti-Semitic ones, in which the joke always made the Jew look like a fool, which he didn't mind playing. He had used his natural smarts to become a salesman whom the Irish loved because he was their "only Jew friend."

If you walked into his enormous office at Ace Builders Supply, which overlooked the East River, you would have seen huge portraits of the pope and the cardinals on his walls, all signed to "Sidney." If the building-material business in New York City had been Tibetan, he would have had huge pictures of Buddah, but since it was Irish, he let everyone know that he had a bunch of buddies who were cardinals. He even appeared in the St. Patrick's Day parade, whereas Yom Kippur was nothing to him but a day to not shave and not eat, to scan the papers and itch to go back to work. Yes, he was a super salesman who knew how to tell just the right dirty j oke. He learned early on that you can amass a fortune by making people laugh about the things they are most ashamed of, such as their libidinous desires.

I remember when I was seven, just before my parents divorced, my father taught me this dirty joke: "What did one broom say to another?"

I had to be a good girl and say, "What, Daddy?"

"How did I get here?" he said. I waited for the punch line, because my old man was the king of shtick: "Your mommy and I swept together."

Even at seven, I got it. I laughed and laughed and ran to tell my mother my new joke, only to have my mouth washed out with soap and hear her scream at my father, "Sidney, don't you ever tell my daughter a filthy joke like that again. She'll tell it to her friends at school, and that will embarrass us." What she didn't know was that my daddy was also the king of embarrassment, and the more he embarrassed my mother, the more he laughed and enjoyed shocking her.

Right before the divorce, the Schumers, her parents, visited us in Riverdale, and Sidney came down the stairs carrying a huge burlesque fan, a prop, which he waved in front of his in-laws, only to be revealed as totally naked. They hated him for being an embarrassment. That was something strange in his psyche: he hated to be humiliated, and yet at the same time he loved to embarrass others. One thing was for certain, though: the night of the big dinner-dance at the Waldorf, he wanted to appear not like a Jewish comedian schlock-monger with jokes about farts and pussies and getting fucked in the ass. No. He wanted to be all dressed up—wearing his Karsh-photograph face and his Hermes tie—and play the part of the wealthy gentleman who was the founder and president of Ace Builders, the largest building-supply company in the world. And he wanted to show off his beautiful daughter, who spoke French and was going to one day inherit the whole lot: his two hotels, his portfolio of deals, and his expanding building-material business. This trophy child was all dressed up and about to play her part in order to please her father—not because she *had* to, but because she wanted to. I braced myself for the cement ball, where my father planned to have his Jewish Cinderella meet his chosen Prince Charming.

My father beamed as he sat on the dais next to Averell Harriman. The band struck up a foxtrot. Already planted in the mind of Irving Menash, who worked as an administrator at the hospital where my father served as president of the board and had a wing named after him, was the idea that his nephew, Mike, a desirable young Jewish bachelor who had graduated from Princeton, should ask me to dance.

Mike trotted over to my table and said, quite seriously, "Good evening, Miss Hochman. My uncle has asked me to dance with you." I had the blush of a fraud since I wasn't Miss Hochman anymore but Madame Shomsky, married to an

71

impoverished, aging Israeli violinist fiddling away somewhere for his supper in Austria. I accepted.

On the dance floor, Mike got immediately to the point. "I've graduated from Princeton and I'm working in my father's law office. I hate it, but it's secure. I actually wanted to be an actor, but that was forbidden, so here I am. My uncle thinks the merging of our families would be a grand idea."

I tried to smile. It was the worst idea I could think of. Mike was sincere and eager. I couldn't wait for the dance to end. Mike insisted on getting my phone number, and I mixed the numbers up so I would never have to talk to him again.

My next swain was Russell Bolin, whose name was originally Bolinovsky, and whose father was a garmento. Mrs. Bolinevsky, who had big ambitions for her son, had paid for him to have his ears tucked and his nose fixed, his teeth capped, and for him to study in Europe. He had savoir faire and was charming. He admitted that he had married a princess, not Jewish, from Spain who had wound up in a mental hospital. He was now divorced and looking for a nice Jewish girl to marry and with whom he could have a family. He wanted nothing less than a townhouse in New York and a house in Pound Ridge. His mother had obviously set her sights on Sidney to finance all this, with me as the sacrificial breeding lamb.

As we danced, I found the cologne Russell was wearing so sweet that I almost fainted. He was a good dancer, and I couldn't help but notice that he had perfect teeth, all capped. He might have been fun a long time ago, before all the fixing and the marriage to the Spanish princess, but he now seemed desperately unhappy. Even Shomsky was beginning to look good compared to all these overachieving lawyers and investment bankers and their social-climbing uncles and mothers.

Soon the music stopped and it was time for the speeches. Averell Harriman, a total gentleman with a bit of Waspy Oyster Bay lockjaw, introduced Sidney as one of the pillars of the financial community. Great applause. Then the pillar, Sidney, spoke. This evening made up for the bar mitzvah his mother couldn't afford and the huge wedding I never allowed him to throw for me. He was, for the moment, a star. Aunt Jewel had coached him in his speech. He was falsely modest and spoke slowly, hiding his New York accent by pronouncing every word carefully. He ended with a folksy "thanks a lot" and accepted a plaque the way actors accept an Oscar. He had had his big moment, and I was there to love him and be proud of him, and that was all he really wanted in life. Woof woof. He was happy.

I was miserable. The next day, Shomsky called and I gave him the news: I would try our marriage again. My father came into my room wearing his frayed bathrobe and seeming hysterically manic, as if he had just heard about the bombing of Hiroshima. I couldn't help but think how great he would have been in the Yiddish theater.

"I saw you dancing with Mike. Do you know what a catch he is? Old man Menash is Rockefeller's lawyer. Mike is young and ambitious, and I can get you a divorce, or better yet an annulment, in a jiffy. I know every judge in this city. As Mrs. Menash, you'll never have a day of worry. I'll set you up, bubbala, like you won't believe. Nothing will be too good for you. You'll have children and I'll finally have grandchildren. Little Menashes, and I'll love them and give them everything money can buy. Mike is the person God sent to you. You should be the happiest girl on Earth. He liked you. I could tell from the dais. I watched you."

"He's not for me, Daddy," I said simply.

I was "throwing salt in his wounds." His whole life was a wound and I was the salt. I was a poet, not a suburban wannabee. I had run off with a pauper who was a failed but

73

great musician. I had chosen to live in poverty in Paris rather than in a suburban palace or, better yet, a townhouse on the Upper East Side, where my decorator would provide me with exciting wallpaper for the guest bathroom.

"Please, please get real, Daddy. I couldn't live with either of those jerks."

"And why not? Well, Russell might be more your type. He lived in Europe. He has an enormous job in his investment firm with clients you wouldn't believe. He's a patron of the Philharmonic, just right for you. You can be a patron, not standing in the wings waiting for some schmuck to stop fiddling."

"What's wrong with those people who are more your type?" asked Aunt Jewel, who had joined us. She wanted to win points by showing Sidney she was on his side.

"Liar," I shot back. "Oh, Daddy, it's so pathetic that you're a control freak and want your name in lights. But leave me out of it."

"That's a way to talk to your father? The man who gave you life? Education? Everything?"

"Daddy, I remember when I was a little girl, you had just given a million dollars to your hospital so they could name a wing after you. You told them that every time anyone in the hospital—anyone—answered the phone, they had to answer, 'The Sidney Hochman Wing,' or they wouldn't get all the money, which was going to be donated over the course of a few years. And I remember you were so crazy as to call the hospital every morning, and if whoever answered the phone said, 'Hello' instead of 'the Sidney Hochman Wing, good morning,' you would raise hell that the phone had to be answered correctly. And you called every day. Just like the time you were appointed the commissioner for the blind for the state of New York. You monitored television programs, and if they dared use the words 'blind to this' or 'blind to that,' you would call the White House and actually tell the president to close down the network because they were insulting the handicapped. You have to be a big shot. And you want me to be part of your image. But I won't be. You can love me. As I love you. But you can't control me. I've made up my mind I'm going back to Shomsky."

"You do that and I'll have a heart attack."

"Please, get another scriptwriter. You know how many times I've heard that you're having a heart attack?"

"You have no heart. In my generation, children respected their parents. This is all from studying Darwin at the fucking Cherry Lawn School I never should have sent you to."

Aunt Jewel tried to introduce a moment of rationality into this overly Jewish discussion. "Darling, what was wrong with those fellows? At least they make a living."

"That's right," Daddy chimed in. "And if you think I'm giving one penny of my hard-earned money to that no-good violinist to support his nothing career, think again, Sandra."

"What's *wrong* with them?" I repeated gently to Aunt Jewel. "They are both ordinary, that's what. And both of those guys I danced with are closet queens," I said with certainty in my voice.

"So what?" screamed my father. "Shomsky is a fairy too. Everyone today is queer. There are no men anymore. That went out with the battle of Normandy and the five-cent subway ride. I hear all the guys are homosexual today. I read it in the papers."

"You never read papers. Your secretary reads them for you."

"Well, all the men today aren't men. But if you're going to go for a queer, why not a rich queer?"

"Your father's right," said Aunt Jewel. "It's easier to love a rich fairy than a poor fairy."

"Stop it, both of you!" I screamed. "I'm not going to be a nice Jewish girl married to a queer with money credentials. I'm not even sure I want to be married. Why do I need a man to validate me? I don't want children. There are enough unwanted children in the world. For God's sake, I was an unwanted child. Do I want to bring into the world more miserable little beings like I was, who get shoved off to boarding school? What's so great about coming into this world, anyway?"

"Shaaa! Stop that! *I* wanted you. I want you now. What other world is there to come into?"

"He has a point," said Aunt Jewel, waxing philosophic.

"Daddy, I'm all fucked up. I don't know who I am. I think I want to be a writer, but I have no idea if I can write. Shomsky has a great talent and he hasn't had the breaks. During the war he worked in a factory and almost ruined his hands. Afterward he played all over England to factory workers, and even went to Zululand to concertize for poor starving black children."

"I wish he'd stayed in Zululand. That's where he belongs. He doesn't know where he belongs. He belongs with the Zulus. They appreciate music. But not with my daughter. Do you know what your education cost me? Cherry Lawn? Twenty thousand dollars a year for nine years. Art camps? Ten grand every summer without an allowance. Bennington? Thirty-two grand a year plus books. All this money put in a shredder. So you could have the life you have. Holding the hat while some fiddler looks for money."

"He's not on the street, Daddy."

"Well, if he's not, he should be. You know, I even thought of taking a contract out on him. That's how much I love my son-in-law the klezmer. I could murder him for what he did to you."

"What did he do?"

"He moved you to Europe. Away from me. That's what he did. When I die, you won't even be here."

"You're not dying. And if you're ever sick, you're only a plane ride away. Don't forget that."

He started crying again. I felt his pain. I remembered when I was a child and it came time for my mother to take me

76

to the train station so I could be shipped off to Cherry Lawn Boarding School. I screamed, "Don't leave me, Mommy!" And now my father, who had always loved me in his own way, was begging me to stay with him. As crazy and emotional as he was, I still loved him. I just couldn't be the person he wanted me to be. I had no idea what person I wanted to be myself. Perhaps I was making another mistake. I should probably be putting down roots. It wasn't as if I had found nirvana with Shomsky. In a way, I didn't know what path to take. I was on such a confusing, absurd journey called life, where other people seemed to know where they were going but I had no idea.

"I have to go to Paris and work things out," I said gently. "But I promise, Daddy, I'll be back soon."

I realized in that moment that I had always been *his* mother, not his child. It was I who had listened to his miseries when he had felt suicidal. He had always dreamed of my growing up to be his little housekeeper, and now I was more or less grown up and was leaving him again. I wished with all my heart I could take away his pain. And that was the absurdly sad part of life: nobody could take away anybody else's pain. Why did people want to own other people's lives?

Sidney tried one more time to keep me from taking the plane back to Paris. "Look, Sandra, remember when I visited you a few months ago in Paris? I didn't tell you, but I saw your beloved husband groping that friend of yours, Milly, who plays the piano. He's definitely shtupping her. I know. I'm a man. That's a *husband?*"

"But my gut tells me I still love him, Daddy."

"Love, schmuv. There's no such thing with a loser like that. I have a whole financial world to leave to you. You have the smarts to run my business. I need you. I really need you with me. You're going to end up divorcing him sooner or later. Why wait till later?"

"I miss my life in Paris, Daddy. I don't feel I belong in America."

"Why not? It's our country."

"No, Paris is where I feel I belong. I have to give our marriage another try. I'll never forgive myself if I don't. Please understand."

While I said good-bye to my daddy at the airport, all the images I had ever written down of how much I loved him ran through my mind. He was a "diamond in the rough," as Aunt Jewel called him. But he *was* a diamond. On the airplane, I thought of how much I adored him. I didn't want to hurt him. He had been hurt enough by my mother. By life. I loved him, but I suspected I still loved Shomsky more than I loved my father.

3.

Returning to Paris

One of the things I learned was that familiarity breeds contempt. Shomsky met me at the airport and we took a cab back to Paris. On the drive, I noticed the beauty of the city. It was lit up and seductive. But Shomsky was anything but seductive. He was petulant. Nevertheless, I was glad I'd come back.

He had begged me to return, and now I was back. This seemed to make him less than overjoyed. I remembered how, just a few years before, I had stared at his beautiful, almost Greek, profile and felt so proud that he had chosen me to love. I wondered how those emotions of excitement and sexual thrill could have evaporated even though he was still the same man. It was hard to believe that I had once been elated to be with him. What I hoped for now was at least friendship. I nursed a nostalgic wish that our history of going through so much would keep us caring for each other.

I wanted to cry as we rode toward the apartment in Montparnasse.

"I'm happy you've come home," Shomsky said, trying to be gay when I could see that he was depressed. My father's apartment wasn't my home, but the apartment in Montparnasse wasn't either. I was an exile in France, a stranger in New York, and I knew from the pain in my stomach that because I'd made the decision to make our marriage work, I might have to force it to happen. Our trip to Greece had turned out to be a nightmare, not a second honeymoon. We had fought all the time. And my trip to New York made me very unsure if I was doing the right thing by leaving Shomsky, because there were many advantages to our marriage. But if I stayed with Shomsky, would I cheat on him again because he didn't satisfy me in bed? No, I would never cheat again. And yet I knew that you couldn't force anything to happen, really. That all we were in control of was ourselves. While Shomsky paid the cab fare, I took a deep breath in the hot summer air. I was going to be a better wife, I promised myself.

Shomsky unlocked the door to our apartment. Oh my God! It was a mess. His clothes on the floor, filthy dishes in the sink. I went upstairs to where we shared a closet, unpacked my suitcase, and began cleaning. It was late. While I cleaned, Shomsky practiced the Sibelius violin concerto that he was engaged to play in Athens in the fall. Finally, once I'd finished waxing the floor, I sat down, all sweaty, to relax. I had found an open bottle of red wine in the kitchen and poured myself a glass. I was at least proud of my handiwork. Our apartment was spotless, and the wooden table that we ate on glowed from furniture polish. Shomsky burst out, almost screaming, "I have my wife back! I'm the luckiest man alive!"

It occurred to me that I was back in my mothering role, taking care of an enormous child who thought the world centered on his needs. I knew that if I needed companionship, I had to make an effort to stop being only Madame Shomsky and dig up my own friends. But it was very hard to meet anyone since Shomsky's attitude was always "Is he [or she] good for my career or bad for my career?" If it wasn't some kind of "contact" who could advance his concert-artist obsession, he wouldn't bother taking an interest in anyone I liked. Shomsky had taught me that opportunism was the name of the game. As if he could read my mind, he said, "Now that you're back, I want you to make yourself useful."

The second week after my return, Shomsky said, "I have a wonderful surprise for you. David Oistrakh is coming to town. And the Soviet embassy has chosen me to entertain him after his concert. It's a real honor. So we're going to be giving a party. I want you to know that the whole musical world will be coming through these doors."

"With what money are we going to do all this?"

He looked manic. "Your friend Peggy Peterson at the American embassy said she would help us. She'll get everything from the PX. I ran into her yesterday at a concert and told her we were ending our separation. She promised to 'liberate' caviar and champagne for the party."

"You mean you asked her to steal things?"

"You see, that's what is wrong with you. You're so hopelessly bourgeois. America is a rich country. The PX is not going to miss a few fish eggs and some bubbly. It's for Soviet-American relations. Nobody has to know."

"She can get fired."

"Don't be absurd. Her father is a congressman. Everything is nepotism. They won't fire her, and she's as excited about the party as I am. Let's get some shut-eye, and tomorrow we'll start making lists."

"Of what?"

"Of guests. And food. I want everything to be very Russian so David will feel at home. Heifetz told me he's dying to meet me. He listens to my Vox recording of the Bartók and tries to imitate my bowing. This ought to help us get concerts. God knows, we need them. We're poor as poor can be. This party will be a shot in the arm."

All right, you idiot, I said to myself. *Shomsky wooed you back to Paris to be his hostess and party planner.* But for a moment I felt glad that I had something to do that would make Shomsky happy for a change and bring him the concerts he deserved. He suffered when he wasn't playing and became bitter about all the second-rate violinists with huge careers because they had money behind them or the right management.

His friend Isaac Stern, who had promised to get him a contract with Hurok Management, had betrayed him and was so obviously jealous of him that they were no longer on speaking terms. Victor Borge had tried to persuade Columbia Artists to take Shomsky on as one of the violinists they booked across America, but in the end, even though Columbia owed Borge a favor since he had made a fortune for them with his classical musical–comedy act, the president of Columbia Artists nixed Shomsky. They already handled two concert-violinist stars. Shomsky had appeared on a primetime television show, where he had been introduced as Heifetz's disciple and favorite violinist. He'd been on *The Ed Sullivan Show* several times. Still, no manager had picked him up. In the concert business, as a performer without a manager you're dead. It's worse than being an actor without an agent, because an actor without an agent can still hear about parts through the grapevine or the Equity bulletin board or some showbiz newspaper, and audition. But as far as concert violinists are concerned, there are only a handful who make a killing, and those are the stars with big managers.

How I hated the people at the Hurok office, who were like toadies at a court. Hurok was the king, and for him to actually take your call meant you were a gold mine or he needed you in some way. Managers were famous for "not taking calls" or for putting you on hold. Once when I had called the great big fat slob Hurok himself, under the guise of being a reporter for the *New York Times* (he was, as all managers are, a glutton for press coverage), he had actually picked up the phone and said "Hello" to me. When I explained that as well as being a journalist I was managing Shomsky, it registered that a nobody—in other words, me—was calling, and he hung up the phone, slamming it down in my face.

For managers, the phone was their weapon, and ignoring calls gave them the power they so badly craved. With few exceptions, every manager I had ever met was a nontalent who lived off his clients' successes. They were star fuckers with the power to be gatekeepers to the stars. I often thought that if I had the money, I would throw a huge manager's ball and invite all the agents and managers to come dressed up as their favorite clients. Hurok the great would probably come as Isaac Stern, complete with big belly, bad taste, and a Stradivarius.

Still, I hoped that Shomsky *would* find a manager who could book him in Europe. God knows we ass-kissed enough patrons and conductors. Every time we went to a concert, it was not to hear the music ("Music? Who likes music?") but to promote or flatter some asshole high on the totem pole of concertania who had the power to book concert artists.

Agents and bookers in my opinion were the lowest of the low, even lower-class than most managers, and the only thing they had in common was that they were all crooks who were out to exploit the artists and cook the books. If you were as successful as Milstein or Mischa Elman or Heifetz, managers would do everything for you: book concerts, arrange for massages, even pimp for you if you needed pimping. Most male concert artists did not need a pimp; they were considered as glamorous as movie stars, and dozens of women ran up to them in the green room or even on the streets. If they were stars, the women groupies (or the men groupies) would throw themselves at them and beg to be their lover. Conductors, like Bernstein, where in the same category.

Shomsky was not yet in that category, but there were plenty of old dames competing for his attention, not to mention the attention of his penis, and the dozens of groupies were one of the reasons I had left him in the first place. My husband was starved for attention, and those women were fuckables starved for someone in the limelight with talent or "genius" to recognize *them*. Shomsky, I believed, used his concertizing as his sexual calling card. Of all the violinists, Heifetz was the only one I'd met who had dignity and didn't do that. Instead, he spent most of his time holed up in Los Angeles snubbing the concert world.

Of all Shomsky's colleagues, only two mensches helped him get concert bookings. They were Ruggiero Ricci, who was friendly and down to earth, and Sasha Schneider, from the Budapest String Quartet, who was a skirt-chasing charmer with Renaissance taste. Schneider cared more about art than music and was always generous and in touch with people to help artists get into "the club". He considered Shomsky a genius who hadn't received the breaks he deserved.

I was realizing that being a musical "performer" seemed glamorous on the outside, but was nightmarish, competitive, and back-stabbing on the inside. It was a terrible world of disappointments, low-lifes, and wannabees, and, for us at any rate, of near-poverty. Shomsky had missed the mark of rationality when he thought my father would be his proud money machine, basking in the glory of rubbing shoulders with concert artists. But Sidney had no desire to meet Glenn Gould or Eugene Ormandy and didn't even know who they were. He was a man who knew about cement, not cadenzas. In that regard, Shomsky had certainly missed the boat when he married me. He had had his pick of movie stars and wealthy Jewish girls, and he secretly held a grudge because Sidney wouldn't spring for a Stradivarius violin. He wouldn't even give us an allowance of more than two hundred dollars a month, when what we really needed was two thousand to survive in the right circles and avoid being beggars.

We lived hand-to-mouth, constantly pretending that we weren't broke, and trying to keep up with the Rothschilds instead of the Joneses. Now we were planning a "promote the career" party for Oistrakh. I was ashamed to have people come to our duplex apartment and see holes in my bedspread, furniture that was mended with patches, towels that were beyond frayed.

"Shomsky, you're nuts to invite a lot of people to come here. This place is pathetic," I said.

"Nonsense. The rich love to see bohemians suffer. It makes them feel good. Besides, we have plenty of linen that the original owners left behind. We can cover everything, the tables and furniture, with white linen. It will look very elegant and very summery," he said. He was excited about the party.

"I don't know, Shomsky. That's what they do in religious Jewish homes when people die."

He laughed. "Don't worry. It's the company that's important. And you're such a good cook, they'll be impressed with the food. And free champagne? Nobody has to know it was stolen."

The next day, I met with Peggy at the American embassy and shuddered at the thought that she was putting her job on the line to steal liquor and food for our party. We went to the Deux Magots to have coffee and discuss how to manage the whole event.

"Shomsky is telephoning everyone in the music world and the French society world to invite them," I told Peggy. "This is the first time the Russians are allowing one of their great artists to be entertained by Westerners. So many of them have defected. I hear that Oistrakh is coming with his KGB bodyguards."

"How exciting," Peggy said. She added, "I really can't stand Shomsky because I think he's a conceited ass who treats you terribly, but since I love you and you decided to go back to him—God only knows why—we might as well do this thing right."

But "right" wasn't going to be cheap. Peggy stuffed two rolled-up American hundred-dollar bills into my hand.

"Don't be silly," I said, trying to hand them back.

"I'm not silly. I can afford it. My father, unlike yours, sends me a huge allowance, and money is meant for friends to be happy. You'll give it back to me one day when Shomsky is the next Menuhin. Everyone wants to meet Oistrakh, even people who hate the violin, because he's such a musical superstar. Now listen. Neither of us will be going to the concert. We can listen to him on a record, so it doesn't matter. We have to prepare to be servants." "Don't forget to invite the American literary stars: Jimmy Baldwin, James Jones, George Plimpton, and a few beatniks for local color," Peggy said.

We were almost like two little girls playing grown-up. The Russian embassy had invitations printed at Cartier. Their list included many of the great and glamorous names in music, as well as many celebrities who would be at the concert, such as the First Lady, Jacqueline Kennedy, Henry and Clare Boothe Luce, the Rothschilds, film stars, and dignitaries from the Russian embassy.

"Peggy, my house is the house of a pauper. What am I going to serve? How am I going to pull all this together and make it elegant, or at least not a catastrophe?"

"We'll do it, we'll do it," she assured me. Peggy was not high on being a general for what I called the pauper's gala. "We must serve Russian food."

"I have no idea how to cook Russian food. My grand-mother, who was from Odessa, used to make borscht. And several times at the Russian Tea Room in New York I had blini, but that's it."

"Blini. That's brilliant," she said. Blini are small pancakes served with caviar and dollops of sour cream. "I can get pancake mix from the PX. We have the caviar, no problem, and I can easily liberate sour cream. What you have to do, Sandra, is go right away to the Rue des Rosiers, that's in the old part of the city, where they sell beets. Borscht is a snap. It's just beet juice. I can borrow little cups from the embassy, and we can be different and serve borscht with champagne. I'll be the maid. I can easily buy a maid's uniform, get a silver tray, and we can serve cups of borscht like demitasse, and blini and caviar as finger food on small plates with cocktail napkins and fish forks."

"It sounds messy. And where will everyone sit? We have no furniture. No small tables."

"That's no problem," said Peggy with wild-eyed enthusiasm, now rising to her adopted role of event planner. "I'll rent folding chairs and stools, and we can set them up around your loft living room. We'll put candles all over the place. I'll get one of the interns from the embassy to play butler. I know just the guy. I'll rent him a costume too. With candles and flowers, it will be divine."

"Flowers? Who has money for flowers?"

"Don't laugh, but there's a funeral parlor right near the embassy, and the doorman is my friend. I slip him a few bucks and he always gives me fresh flowers right after a funeral. I'll ask him to give us loads of flowers. I have lots of vases, and I'll arrange them myself."

"Really? How do you know there'll be a funeral that day? We can't have wilted flowers."

"In Paris there's *always* a funeral, silly. Leave it to me. Now, use the cash I gave you to buy yourself a decent dress, because this is going to be the party of the year. Also some shoes. And get your hair done. Don't forget to buy a lot of beets, and I'll take care of the rest." She smiled. "I spoke on your behalf to the man at the embassy who's handling all the Oistrakh publicity, and he said the concert is sold out and people are paying all sorts of ridiculous prices to get in. I asked how many people were coming, and he said forty-five celebrities are coming from all over the world."

"Oh my God. How can I cook forty-five blini?"

"Don't worry. You'll do fine. Just don't put on any background music unless it's jazz, because you don't want to offend any of the musicians. If Shostakovich is coming, he doesn't want to walk into a room where they're playing Stravinsky, if you know what I mean. Oistrakh is playing the Sibelius violin concerto, so you might put on some soft Sibelius in the background, but not the violin concerto, all right? Let's make this shindig rock."

When I went to the Rue des Rosiers, the Jewish part of town, to buy beets for my borscht, I learned that for some arcane reason, only cooked beets—beets already boiled—were sold in Paris. In no market anywhere, I was told by a vendor in French, could I buy raw beets. It was the day of the party, and I was desperate to make everything Russian. For a moment I thought of buying borscht from the most elegant Russian restaurant in Paris, Domonics, but that would be wildly expensive, and I already had spent Peggy's cash on a pretty and simple black satin dress and expensive high heels. I bought the cooked beets and hauled them in my fishnet bag back to our apartment to cook them again. I decided to make the best of the borscht situation.

When I got home, Shomsky was already dressed in a tux and was getting ready to go to the concert in a limousine provided by the Russian embassy. He was very excited about being chosen to be Oistrakh's host from all the swanky musicians who would have died to be giving the after-concert party. He knew this would make him look like a celebrity to the whole music world and give him the kind of standing in the music community that would help him get international bookings. I kissed him, and, before I got dressed, I went into the kitchen.

The pretend-to-be butler was opening champagne. Peggy, in her starched white uniform with a snood on her hair and a lacy apron, looked like a true domestic. Shomsky warned us before he left not to set the house on fire with all the candles and to be sure to have everything ready in two hours, when the concert would be over. It was a warm summer night, and the apartment, filled with great bunches of funereal white gladioli, white roses, and white azaleas, and with all the ragged furniture and the poor bed covered in white starched sheets, looked as elegant as a stage set.

We began Operation Borscht and soon realized that the beets weren't throwing off their juice in the huge pot that we were using to reboil them. The water, instead of bubbling bright pink, looked slightly orange. The borscht wasn't working.

"Here," said Peggy with a grin. She poured ketchup she had taken from the embassy into the pot. "This gives it the right color."

I started to make the blini. "Oh my God!" I screamed, tasting one of the small pancakes I had made from the Aunt Jemima pancake mix. "These taste like shoe leather! They're disgusting."

"Oh, don't be such a perfectionist, Sandra. Who cares? People are coming to meet Oistrakh. They don't give a shit about the food. They will be fine. Go upstairs. Take a bubble bath and get dressed."

Fifty small pancakes later, I did as she ordered. The pancakes tasted like small hand grenades, but it was too late. I just hoped no one would be very hungry.

*   *   *

The door burst open. Two bodyguards arrived, carrying guns and speaking Russian. The butler served the best champagne, and the party began.

I didn't feel gay or bubbling over with the kind of joy the hostess of such a grand event should have felt. A lot of strangers and acquaintances, who were really snobby freeloaders, were invading my house. And why? To celebrate after a concert that was just another public-relations event for Shomsky. Perhaps, I thought warily, every party is some sort of self-promotion. A shot at making others feel you're something that you're not. I was not filled with the pleasure of hospitality. I was anxious that our party not be a flop. But when I saw my dear friend Peggy working her buns off in the kitchen trying to help me look prosperous out of the goodness of her heart, I started to feel giddy and excited.

The show of appearances was pathetic. Peggy knew how broke we were and that Shomsky had recently begged his violinmaker to loan us some money so the phone wouldn't be turned off—but her attitude was "on with the show." Usually we had to scrounge for taxi money or cheap food while surrounded by people with loads of money for whom Paris was a constant party. Now, of course, it was too late to think of that.

Suddenly, in came the beaming, fat David Oistrakh, flush from a great concert. He was followed by two equally fat Russians from the embassy who were schlepping the great man's violin. He was also followed by Stravinsky, the old wizard, and some young friend of his. As my husband, animated and proud, came to the door, he was talking to the short and bald and very ancient Virgil Thomson. Some society patrons, gabbing away in French about the beauty of the music, were followed by the tuxedo-clad chairman of Time-Life, Henry Luce, with his glamorous wife, Clare. It was rumored that they were visiting Paris because they wanted Oistrakh for the cover of *Time*. Soon, on one of the hottest evenings of the summer, more patrons, including the Baron and Baroness de Rothschild, filtered in to the party. People had flown in for the concert from all over the world.

I admired Clare Boothe Luce, not particularly for her politics, which as the world knew were Republican, but for her witty play *The Women*, which had been such a success on Broadway and which I adored as both a play and a film. Mrs. Luce seemed to me to be the essence of glamour and wit, all those smart-set women she had written about rolled into one. The society housewife, the trampy social climber, the long-suffering mother—they were all Clare Boothe Luce. Even though she bleached her hair blond and obviously had had her nose fixed, she was elegant and witty, and you could see on her face that being married to the leading media tycoon of the world was no day at the beach. Hers was a world of New York, Hawaii, London, Paris, and Southern chic, billion-dollar corporations, and Washington and Georgetown politics. It was said about her that if you blindfolded her and put her in a room filled with people, she could sniff out the most powerful man in the room.

She was both grande dame and Oscar Wilde-ish. It was said that she, not George Bernard Shaw, had come up with the witty line "No good turn goes unpunished," which I often thought of as one of the most brilliant one-liners ever. She had also been quoted as saying "Home is where you hang your architect." As she stood elegantly in my Parisian apartment, where I was a glorified house sitter so that Shomsky and I could survive without paying rent, she graciously approached me. She said, "Sandra, you are such a beauty. The concert was frankly a bore, but this party is the most fun I've had in ages. Where did you find all these beautiful white azaleas? They're my favorite flowers."

"At a funeral parlor," I said.

"Brilliant," she said.

I thought it was amazing that she and Mr. Luce had gone to the concert, since they wrote constantly about how they detested communists. I knew that she and her husband believed in the idea of the American Century, the anthem and the flag, manifest destiny and significant ideas. As a student of history at Cherry Lawn who had followed current events since the age of nine, I knew she had addressed the Republican Convention and called Roosevelt's second vice president, Henry Wallace, "Stalin's Mortimer Snerd" and Wallace's ideas "Globaloney." Here was Mr. Luce, someone who chased after communists and reigned over Time-Life's conservative empire, rubbing shoulders with one of the Soviet Union's most celebrated communists, David Oistrakh. True to form, Mrs. Luce headed straight to the star himself and began a conversation that was translated by his KGB bodyguards into Russian. As the two stood sipping champagne together, a big smile grew on Oistrakh's face.

Many more boisterous guests came pouring through our door. It was the Paris film crowd, who, like wolves, always traveled in a pack. Shomsky promoted them constantly since, as a frustrated actor, he was hoping to appear in a *nouvelle cinéma* film. We went religiously to the Cinémathèque to see the new-wave films of Vadim, Godard, Truffaut, and Polanski.

Vadim, it turned out, was a great music lover and had us over to his apartment, where Shomsky played a concert personally for him. He would say, "Shomsky, you have the musical talent of a god and the personality of a movie star, and I'm going to put you in my next film." That always made my husband happy and put him in a good mood.

Polanski, whose film *Knife in the Water* had shocked everyone and been the rage of Parisian cinema, sat huddled in a corner talking to the young American film star Jean Seberg and to his friend and competitor Jean-Luc Godard. Richard Kaplan, a young, handsome American and the scion of the Welch's grape juice family, was there with his girlfriend, the model Ivy Nicholson.

Shostakovich arrived soon after, and I led him to David Oistrakh, whom he kissed on both cheeks. I had heard that Shostakovich and Stravinsky were enemies since Shostakovich was a true communist who touted the party line and Stravinsky, who lived in Paris, hated communism and had defected from his motherland as soon as he could. I made a mental note to make sure they were always at opposite ends of the room.

Soon everyone was sipping our bright red borscht out of demitasse cups from the embassy. Peggy had cleverly, I thought, used white-out to cover the American seal so that no one thought this was a party where the host and hostess couldn't afford their own china. Of course, paper cups wouldn't do. Our fake butler poured champagne into the heavy crystal flutes left behind by the apartment owners with assurances that we were welcome to use them. I observed with horror that when the inexperienced young man poured champagne, he chipped the rim of each flute. I wanted to close my eyes and not even think about the fact that one of the immortals at the party could swallow some tiny chip of glass and drop dead and I might be arrested for murder. But everyone seemed to be tactfully positioning their glasses to avoid the chipped spots. I realized that I might be worrying beyond reason.

Peggy drew me into a corner. "The party is divine. It was so clever of Shomsky to invite his butcher and his barber and that old lady from the pastry store, all of whom speak Russian. They loved the concert, and Oistrakh is so enjoying chatting with them in his own language. Don't you see? This party is a huge success because it has people of all colors and classes, the knowns and the unknowns, which is what only an artist can pull off. Paris is so class-conscious. Shomsky is one of the few people who know everyone from every corner of the city, from the richest baroness to the *clochards* under the bridges."

I saw the ambassador from Kenya, who had come in full African dress, talking about music and his adoration of the violin with Jacqueline Kennedy, who had arrived late and so discreetly that most people hardly knew she was there. She was accompanied by her own Secret Service guards. Clustered around the First Lady were many of the musicians who came into and out of our lives in Paris, although none of them had ever been invited to our humble home, which now didn't seem quite so humble with white sheets over everything, candlelight, and hundreds of white flowers perfuming the room.

The pianists Sigi Weissenberg and Julius Katchen, who despised each other, were engaged in a phony conversation about how they admired each other's talent. The word *pianissimo* was floating in the air as they smiled at each other and drank their champagne when everyone in the music world knew they bad-mouthed each other's technique at every opportunity.

Nathan Milstein and Mischa Elman had both flown in to Paris for the big event, the concert of the century. I thought to myself, "Oistrakh is cementing international relations through music." Even though the Cold War was at its height, there was a feeling for the moment that music could bridge the gap of hatred that existed between Soviet Russia and the free world. In the candlelight I could see my husband sucking up to the stunning Jacqueline Kennedy. How predictable. Shomsky, of course, was the ultimate self-promoter and star fucker. I could hear Mrs. Kennedy saying in her whispery, baby-doll voice how she had a copy of his recording of the Bartók and how she and the president preferred it to another Bartók recording.

Mrs. Kennedy was radiant and poised and seemed very shy as she told Shomsky how she had come for a quick fitting of some clothes at Balenciaga in Paris, but had stayed an extra day to hear Oistrakh's historic concert. She glided over to

Oistrakh and looked at him with her lovely, wide-set brown eyes. She whispered how, as a young girl at Chapin, she had discovered the poetry of the violin and how much the music meant to her. I knew that President Kennedy didn't give a damn about Bela Bartók, but it was a gracious lie and certainly made my husband feel important for the moment. Then I saw her and her Secret Service men discreetly slip out the door like shadows.

I was relieved that Oistrakh was having a great time. Brigitte Bardot had shown up, and he was apparently involved in explaining through his interpreter how much he admired her films. He was saying that his wife and son, who were back in Moscow, were also fans. Whenever he talked to any of the guests, his bodyguards stayed glued to him.

Many of the guests politely refused my poor little blini, which were being passed around by the make-believe butler, probably because they didn't want to get the runny sour cream and caviar on their elegant clothes. We didn't have the budget for small white linen napkins, and when Peggy suggested paper cocktail napkins, Shomsky had gotten very annoyed at her. "Nobody uses paper napkins at an elegant party in Paris," he said. It was, in his opinion, very déclassé of Peggy to even *suggest* paper napkins. Shomsky's barber, however, helped himself to dozens of blini, not caring if the sour cream got all over his hands—which he cleaned, I observed, by using his trousers as his napkin. Shomsky clinked a fork against a crystal glass, and the guests stopped talking.

"To my friend, David Oistrakh, the greatest violinist in the world and our comrade from Russia, I want to say *merci mille fois* for coming to our home and for the great concert."

This was translated by Oistrakh's bodyguard into Russian, since Shomsky's Russian was not as fluent as he had once bragged that it was. Everyone applauded. It was extraordinary to see Nathan Milstein, Henryk Szeryng, and Yehudi Menuhin all maintain perfect phony smiles when Shomsky lauded Oistrakh as the world's greatest violinist, since each of them secretly believed, without a shadow of a doubt, that *he* was the world's greatest violinist. David Oistrakh, compared to each of them, was just a sloppy émigré from Russia who was receiving all this attention because he was a political tool. (Of course, they did not betray any of their jealousy. That, I knew, would come after the party, when they confided to their wives or mistresses or confidants what a fool Shomsky was to even suggest this in public.)

Oistrakh took a modest bow and replied through his interpreters that he was having such a good time at the party that as a gift to his guests, he would play for them the first movement of the Bruch Concerto no. 1 in G minor. Everyone gasped, as no one expected him to give a special little private concert, and broke into hysterical applause. One of the bodyguards took Oistrakh's priceless Stradivarius out of its green velvet–lined alligator case and held it up as if it were the golden chalice. I was told it was worth five million dollars.

The divine little concert began. Everyone was hushed. Oistrakh bowed the music with rapid passages up and down the strings. As he played, I couldn't help but think of how a maestro like Oistrakh, or Shomsky for that matter, as a wunderkind had had to give up a normal, carefree childhood in order to learn ear training, fingering, and scores, and to become a music machine to compete against other music machines. Playing the violin the way they played was a skill that took a lifetime to learn and the vigilance of practicing every day.

The audience in my living room was in awe of being so close to Oistrakh as he brought magic out of his instrument. Quietly and warmly, Max Bruch's music filled the room with its emotions as everyone was riveted, watching Oistrakh's thick fingers move rapidly up and down the strings to create the perfect sound. When he finished, he held the bow in the air in triumph and everyone applauded madly.

At midnight, the guests began to leave, shaking hands with or hugging Oistrakh and saying a few words in either Russian or French or English. Soon, only Peggy, Shomsky, Oistrakh, and I—and the bodyguards—were left. Oistrakh smiled at me and said a few words to his interpreters. They turned to me and said, "Mister Oistrakh wants you to know, Madame Shomsky, how much he enjoyed the party. This was the best American food he ever tasted."

Peggy and I laughed. Our Russian food had been a flop. But the party had been a huge success. When we were alone, Shomsky hugged me and told me how proud he was of me for having thrown the party of the year. The next day, he answered dozens of calls as people phoned to thank him. His musical stock had risen. And it was wonderful to see him finally smiling.

Over the next few weeks, I felt that my husband and I were growing closer, although he disappeared mysteriously for hours on end, which I suspected meant he was visiting with Miriam, the furrier's wife, who still called our house constantly. I began to think that my husband did care for me and that I was important to him. As a result of word of mouth about the Oistrakh party, we were invited out to dinner by many of the famous concert musicians who had previously ignored us. Most artists preferred to stay in Paris during the summer because it was almost empty, and this summer we could save money because we had so many invitations to dine out. And then an event happened that was to ruin our marriage, which was already in such a delicate state.

Shomsky received a phone call from Raoul Castro, Fidel's brother, who was a major in the Cuban army and who appeared in Paris after the world learned of Cuba Libre, the end of the revolution. Fidel Castro's winning the freedom of his country from Batista appealed to the imagination of the world, and, particularly in Paris, he was a revolutionary hero. Raoul came to call on us. He was dressed in his army uniform, was tall and elegant, and spoke English almost without an accent. Shomsky was very excited to hear what he had to say.

"My dear Shomsky, my brother, Fidel, wants me to invite you to play at the celebration of freedom in Havana next week. It is not just a party but a two-week celebration to which we have invited our comrades from all over the world. I have just spoken with Pablo Picasso, Yves Montand, Simone Signoret, Sartre, Françoise Sagan, and many other artists in France who will be guests of our newly freed country. There will be thousands of guests from all over the world. There will be fireworks, food, dancing, and music to celebrate my brother's courage and the people's liberation from Batista and capitalism. Will you come? We think you and your wife will be very happy with your accommodations and the whole event."

Unlike the pictures of Fidel Castro in khakis and a beret, Raoul looked almost like a toy soldier with many medals and much gold braid on his uniform. He was glamorous and confident, and at the same time self-important. He was humble. He was charming. My husband and I were thrilled to be invited. Since I had been conceived in Cuba, the thought of going there to meet Fidel Castro and Che Guevara and all the great leftists of the world was very appealing. We weren't leftists, but perhaps the party for Oistrakh had jump-started a trend of Shomsky being invited to pro-Russian events. Certainly this was a big honor, to play for thousands of people and President Castro.

I laughed to myself as I listened to Raoul Castro praising the music of Shomsky when the fact was that Shomsky only hung out with the richest, the stupidest, the most right-wing capitalists of the world. He was constantly ass-kissing the

Rothschilds and the man who ran the Levi Strauss company and so many other Americans who headed public companies for whom Castro was poison. But in some strange way Shomsky was a chameleon, and knowing that this celebration would bolster his career, I was overjoyed that we were going to Cuba as guests of Castro himself.

Two days before the trip, Shomsky was practicing his scales, as he usually did in the morning. I was cleaning the table from breakfast. He stopped playing.

"Sandra, sit down. I want to talk to you."

Whenever he said "sit down," I knew trouble was brewing.

"What's up?" I asked.

"You're not going."

"What do you mean?"

"I'm not taking you with me."

"You're kidding me," I said. I felt a clenched fist in my stomach punching me.

"No. You'd be in my way," he said softly.

"In the way? But I go with you everywhere. This is going to be so important for us. It's history."

"No, I want my freedom. I want to meet who I want to meet. Go where I want to go. I don't need a wife like a noose around my neck. I like to be where the action is. I don't want to go as a couple. I want to go alone and not have you share the limelight."

I started to hold my breath to keep from crying. "But I'm your wife."

"I know. But I'm going to Cuba alone. Case closed."

I wanted to cry. But I also knew that if I was cool, it would be better for me later on. I didn't want to give him the satisfaction of seeing what I really felt. I thought, *Fuck you. If I'm good enough to travel third-class to the pit stops of Greece, I should be good enough to be there when the Cuban government invites us as honored guests. And besides, I was invited too.*

"Raoul Castro said there were two tickets," I said.

"I'm only accepting one. You stay here in Paris. It will only be two weeks."

I felt abandoned and angry. I felt humiliated. Rejected. And sad. I knew then that our marriage was over. He thought only of one person: himself. I was a zero.

The Zeros: If a scroll of silk arrives, it may be this letter telling you silence is closer to sleep than poems. (HELP ME) There's a sound inside my dreams close to the shape of zero. In dreams I move in frozen circles looking for the homes I cannot find. (I AM HOMELESS) In dreams I sleep in France in an autobus. I wake up at a place where thatched cottages appear and I'm told they are "inns for the soul." But there's not one place to rent and nowhere to go. (FOLLOW ME) It is then that the secret of sleep resembles the snowflake. It is then I forge nails out of nothing at all. I am hammering my footprints on the grass. I am sleeping inside the curves of the frozen zero. (EVERYWHERE NOISE AWAKENS MY DREAMS)

If I was a huntress of words, it was because I was a huntress of silence. And just as the American Indians went out to trap otter, jackal, swollen pelts of beasts, so I went trapping silence for myself. At night I listened to the fumes, the greased machines. The end of things. When a wheel broke, it was not the wheel of life. Buddha's great wheel of birth and endless death. It was the pierced flat tire of the car. Dying beneath the windows. Silence was always close to me: that moment when I move inside the dream to pierce things.

My childhood house is still a long ribbon of rooms—green and slightly frayed. The food grew on the tables. Florida oranges fell apart in skin thick as a hand. Floors were waxed in darkness, and sunlight shone only in the bathroom and the front bedrooms. There! I look out at the Hudson sailing me into the sun. My own river—color of scum. I see white birds and far away the neverland of cliffs and Palisades. Here tulips blossom in a red brick pot. O, I am out of my crib. I grow like a great bulb too big for where I am cut.

"Do we live here?"

"Foreign wars," says my mother as she walks in high slippers down the corridors.

"Hitler," says my nurse, guarding her pocket money for my toys.

"They make a lot of noise," say the neighbors, stamping on the floors during the evenings when my parents scream.

But I never wake up. It isn't a dream. Turtles are flushed down the toilet and goldfish swim in the large glass bowl where pebbles are larger than teeth.

4.

Harold

Another abandonment.

Shomsky packed. And left for Cuba, promising to call me, if the phones were working, as soon as he arrived in Cuba. He took his suitcase stuffed with summer clothes and sunscreen and disappeared into the elevator. I was alone in Paris.

I sat on our bed and cried. He had left me very little money. Worse than that, I realized that without him around, I had no one to talk to. All our friends were really acquaintances and hangers-on, and without Shomsky at my side they had no reason to talk to me or even see me. Summer. Paris. Loneliness. I faced the fact that outside of Peggy, I had *no* friends, only *contacts*.

The next morning, I rang up Peggy and she promised to meet me one night for dinner so I wouldn't be alone. I was too shy to call anyone else I knew and, I admitted sadly to myself,

I hadn't developed the art of asking people to my house for dinner without sounding pathetic or desperate. I discovered with a shock that without my family in Paris, there was nobody I could turn to. I decided to take myself to my favorite museum, the Museum of Man, near the Trocadéro. Wandering around looking at African masks, I thought of Shomsky and how angry and sad I was that he had dumped me to go to the limelight of Cuba and be festive. I imagined him playing the star and picking up young women with the same spiel he had used to seduce me. *What an idiot I am,* I thought as I looked at an African mask that looked back at me from behind glass.

"You *are* an idiot," the mask said.

Surely I was going crazy. No. I was just *imagining* the mask answering my thoughts with a shaman's echo.

"Sandra."

I turned around. Harold Norse stood in front of me.

"What are you doing here?" he asked. "I haven't seen you since I left New York three years ago and sold all my opera librettos and books and took off for Paris."

"Oh my God, I forgot you were here," I said, grateful to know *anyone.* "Otherwise I would have looked you up."

"Well, here I am! Timing is everything." He had thick black eyebrows and bright blue eyes. He was rumored to be a great poet. I knew he'd had a few books published, but he had been overshadowed by the star Beatnik poets Ginsberg, Corso, Rexroth, Snyder. He must have been about fifty, and he was losing his hair. A line from one of his poems that I had heard at a reading he gave with the poet Howard Hart in Greenwich Village had stayed in my mind like a musical phrase: "If you want to survive I would not recommend love."

"Hey! You can be my beard!" he said. "With you I won't look queer. I'm so glad I met you. There's a whole scene going on here that I bet you're not even aware of. I heard through the grapevine that you married some old violinist. Where is he?"

"Cuba. He went to play the violin at the Cuba Libre celebration and left me behind. I don't really know anyone in Paris except a bunch of upper-class snobs who only have anything to do with me because I'm the wife of Shomsky. Once he goes away, I have almost no one."

"Great! Things are about to change. Things are looking up for you as of this very moment. You and I are going to be an item on the scene, babe."

"How so?"

"Well, you know I'm queer, but I'm not interested in anyone else knowing all that much about me. It's harder to publish your love poems if people know you're writing them to a man, which is crazy. Because most of the great poets were queer, for God's sake. Shakespeare, Marlowe, Rimbaud, Gérard de Nerval, Walt Whitman, Hart Crane—and everybody else, but I don't like to advertise that. I prefer a cool ass to a hot pussy, the way Ginsberg does. But unlike Ginsberg, I'm not sure I want to play the homo ticket. I want to be known as a great American poet, not a great *queer* American poet, and that's where you come in perfectly. You can cover for me. There *is* a God!"

"What are you talking about?"

"Here's the deal. You and I make the scene. Anaïs Nin just laid a lot of bread on me so I could finish my new book without starving to death, à la everybody else I know. She's married to a rich banker called Hugo who's also a lithographer and photographer. See? It figures. And he is so crazy about her, he helps her to help indigent writers become famous. She usually sleeps with everyone she helps, but that's not necessarily her style. She fell in love with Henry Miller and helped him move from a messenger boy to a great literary star. It was all her bread and emotional support. She's rumored to be working on a diary that she's been writing in for years, ever since she was eight years old. Henry Miller told me it's a masterpiece, that it's the greatest writing since Voltaire or Montaigne. She keeps it in a vault, and one day it's going to rock the world. Meanwhile, she publishes her own books with a pedal press. Hugo illustrates them. Novels. Short stories. And every day, she works on her secret diaries. She calls them a 'bridge' to her father."

"Why did she start writing them?" I asked, fascinated by the intensity with which Harold spoke. He had such compulsive energy.

"Her father was the Cuban pianist Joaquin Nin. She adored him, and when her mother took her away from Cuba, she began the diaries as a way of communicating with her absent father to maintain contact with him."

"Why are you telling me all this?" I asked as we walked down the museum halls and out into the streets of Paris.

"Why? Because none other than the great Anaïs Nin is having a book party tonight to launch one of her own books of short stories that she's published herself. And the whole Parisian literary scene, Sandra, is going to be there. Everyone, darling. She's a legend in her own time. But what you don't seem to realize is that there's a whole underground scene going on here. The greatest literary scene since Hemingway and Fitzgerald and Joyce. Right here. In Paris. Under your nose. And you should be part of it with me."

"I've never *heard* of Anaïs Nin."

"Of course not, stupid. They don't teach her at Bennington. She's not part of that academic group of nontalents that rule the literary scene. The pseudocommies whose business it is to keep everybody with any talent from publishing. Do you have any idea of who's here in Paris, right under your nose?"

"No, I don't. I don't know any writers."

"Well, let's rock, baby. There's Jimmy Baldwin, an American genius who's a Negro and walks around Paris totally anonymous. Meanwhile, his essay 'Nobody Knows My Name' was published in the *New Yorker,* in between liquor ads, and woke middle-class America up to the fact that 'black is beautiful' is a myth. It's just one more American myth, like 'the check is in the mail,' or 'I promise I won't cum in your mouth.' The great Jimmy is here, baby, walking the same streets as Lawrence Durrell, Anaïs Nin, Henry Miller, Gregory Corso, William Burroughs. Allen and Peter"—Ginsberg and Orlovsky—"come for visits. Hey man, everyone is *here*. James 'From Here to Eternity' Jones is here living on the Île Saint Louis without a telephone. Is that cool?"

"I know Jimmy Baldwin and James Jones because they came to my party, but I didn't get a chance to actually talk to them."

"Man Ray, the genius of surrealism, painting, and photography, hangs around the Deux Magots with his beautiful wife and writes poems on napkins. None of these dudes go away in the summer. For the *real* artist, Paris rocks in the summer. Ever hear of Pablo Neruda?"

"Of course. He's my favorite poet. *Twenty Love Sonnets and a Song of Despair* are my favorite love poems. My teacher Ben Bellitt at Bennington translated them from Spanish."

"Well, whoop-de-doo! The great man himself is coming to the book signing of Anaïs Nin today. At five o'clock. And you're coming with me. I'm going to be the new Virgil to your female Dante. It's time that Shomsky was told that you are a person with talent. I'm going to introduce you to the whole scene. Man, with your looks and shy personality, Paris is going to be at your feet."

"I'm not so sure," I laughed. "But it would certainly be refreshing to meet some writers and painters for a change." It was the first time I had laughed in months.

"You have no idea the wonders that are awaiting you here in Paris. To begin with, I'm friends with Alain Jouffroy, the leading art critic, and his girlfriend Manina. They have a whole circle of avant-garde artists around them. This is where you belong. With me. With them."

We are in Paris in 1960. Like Hemingway, we are living out the dream.

We went back to my apartment.

"Everyone I know is creating, making trouble, especially Jean-Jacques Lebel."

"Who is this Lebel, exactly?" I asked.

"He's the young spirit of the new avant-garde Paris," Harold said. "He tries to shock and get reactions from the philistines and culture police who are trying to stop real art from happening. He's inventive and creative, and he archives everything he does. Books, happenings, art exhibits, conferences—they're all part of his art form."

"He sounds exciting."

"Believe me, he is. He's nineteen years old. The whole scene is exciting. I'm going to raid your refrigerator while you get dressed for the book signing."

Harold looked as if he hadn't had a good meal in a year. He even stuffed his pockets with cheese and bread as I threw on my long black skirt and black turtleneck. We proceeded to the Anaïs Nin event. It was certainly a change from going to a concert all dressed up like a pet poodle. I was excited to meet the artists and writers I had heard were in Paris but had never gotten to meet or see. They lived in their own circle, and here I was, Sandra Hochman, entering with my guide into this secretive land.

The English bookstore was in the sixth arrondissement near the Church of Saint-Germain-des-Prés. As we entered, I saw dozens of people surrounding a tall, delicately boned woman who might have been in her sixties but seemed ageless. She had obviously had her face lifted, because her skin was the tight flesh of a young girl. Her skin was very white, and she had slanted eyes, a perfect turned-up nose, and smiling, full lips. Her red hair, parted in the middle à la Emily Brontë, was pulled back by a blue velvet ribbon. What was so amazing was her thin, slender body, perfectly formed, the body of a dancer. And even though it was summer, she was wearing a blue velvet dress with puffed sleeves that exposed her long, creamy-white arms. She was signing her book, *Under a Glass Bell and Other Stories,* a slim volume with a gray paper cover, on which appeared a surrealistic engraving by her husband, Ian Hugo, who was nowhere in sight.

Harold explained that they lived part of the time in Paris and the other part of the time in Greenwich Village, in a large apartment complex near University Place. He said that she had also self-published *D. H. Lawrence, An Unprofessional Study,* which Harold claimed was the greatest literary criticism of the twentieth century, as well as a novel called *House of Incest.*

Harold was part genius, part poet, part hustler. In one way, he wanted to help pull me out of my despair and funk, but in another strange way I was a mark. Compared to him, who was practically a vagrant, I had *bread.* He became a squatter in my apartment, but I admit I was grateful for the company. I wasn't alone anymore.

The next day—a bright summer morning—he answered the ringing phone. "It's Pablo Neruda on the phone. The world's greatest poet is calling us. He wants to speak to you, Sandra. Hurry up."

I ran to the phone. "Sandra, my film is showing today at the Chilean embassy. Because of my gout, I can hardly walk. Can you pick Matilde and me up at the hotel and come with us? I want to talk to you. You can be very important for my country."

I got the hotel address and told him I would be there shortly.

Harold thought nothing of going through Shomsky's closet to find a clean pair of socks and a polo shirt, which hung down to his knees. He shaved, and we went to the garage where I kept the car, which my father had given to Shomsky and me as a gift so Shomsky would take me with him on tour. The car was a white English Ford convertible, and I had taken driving lessons and become a very good driver.

When we arrived at the hotel, Pablo was well dressed and Matilde looked like a queen. She had bright red hair and wore a white dress and white kid gloves. They got in the back of the car, with Pablo talking to me as if we were old friends.

I drove quickly. We arrived at the embassy and took our seats in a section of a film theater that was roped off for Neruda and his guests. We were early, and Pablo was shaking hands and chattering away in English with many of his friends who were sitting in the audience.

Harold leaned over and whispered to me, "Do you know this man's story? It's unbelievable." Pablo Neruda's father was a railroad employee who was stationed in the rain forest of Chile, where Pablo grew up loving nature. Pablo went to university and became an ambassador to Rangoon. While working in the diplomatic service he married a Dutch woman. They had a daughter, who died at age eight, after Neruda and his wife had divorced. Witnessing the poverty of the Chilean people inspired Neruda to become a communist. After his first marriage ended, he married a painter, Delia, also a communist, who was much older. The two fled to get away from the witch hunters. After he met Matilde, he built a house in Valparaíso and decided to devote himself to helping humanity. He and Delia divorced but remained friends. At one point he served as consul general to Mexico.

Neruda's poetry is considered by some to be the best of the twentieth century. Harold said, "'Residence on Earth' and his *Twenty Love Sonnets* were written to some stupid woman who rejected him. She had no idea that the greatest Spanish-language love poems of the century were written to her."

Neruda is famous for saying, "If a poem isn't political, it is nothing." And yet his poems are so original. "Ode to My Socks" is typical of the way he could write about *anything* and make it sing. The film we were seeing that night was about the strange ruins of Machu Picchu, in Peru, the subject of one of the poems in what may have been his greatest book, *Canto General*. His work is published in every country in the world.

The lights went out. The documentary film began. The soundtrack of the film was Pablo reciting his poem in Spanish. That was all: the spectacular photographs of the mountain and the sing-song voice of the poet in the background with English subtitles. The whole point of the film, I gathered, was to tell the world that the unknown hands that had created the ruins were now gone. Who were these people? No one knew their names. But they had built, as unknown workers, one of the greatest marvels known to man.

The chanting of the poem in Spanish was a mesmerizing incantation. It was the most fluid combination of image and soundtrack. The voice reciting the poetry and the sound of the music blended with the images. It was a magical retelling of the creation of one of the world's most spiritual and beautiful stone-and-earth monuments.

After the film ended there was great applause. A reception was held at the embassy, to which Harold and I were invited if for no other reason than that I was now Neruda's chauffeur. Pablo buttonholed me. He spoke to me earnestly and with great tenderness.

"I only trust poets. You, Sandra, have come into my life for a reason."

We were all shepherded into a huge, old-fashioned, high-ceilinged ballroom with an enormous chandelier made of delicate crystal. Velvet-covered folding chairs were being set up in rows, and the audience members who had been invited to the film were now quietly taking their seats.

There was to be a reading by the poet himself. A dignified gentleman who spoke excellent English welcomed the guests and, speaking with a slight Spanish accent, addressed us:

> Tonight, I have had the great good fortune to show to an English-speaking audience the brilliant film *Machu Picchu,* which has already been seen by many Spanish-speaking admirers of the great Pablo Neruda. The poetry of Pablo Neruda, mysterious, earthy, passionate, and erotic, seems to surge with irresistible momentum from a bottomless wellspring of intense sexual energy. How can a foundation myth be created in a modern poem? The *Canto General,* from which the Machu Picchu poem is taken, contains various interwoven stories, all of them foundational. One is the history of Latin America from pre-Columbian days to the present. Another is Neruda's own history, his personal life and emergence as a poetic voice; then there is one we could call natural history. All of this you have heard and seen tonight. Critics have attempted to fix the point at which Neruda conceived *Canto General,* as if finding that originary moment would yield a key to a global interpretation of the poem. People have placed the moment of illumination at the time when Neruda climbed to Machu Picchu on his journey home from Mexico in 1943. And now it is my pleasure to present the greatest poet of the twentieth century in my language. In the words of Gabriel García Márquez, "Neruda is a kind of King Midas. Everything he touches turns to poetry."

Neruda got up to thunderous applause. He chose to read in English. "I will only read two short poems. Thank you so much for coming here. It is my hope that one day all nations will speak the language of peace."

Then he began to read in his sonorous voice.

PROMULGATION OF THE FUNNEL LAW

They declared themselves patriots
In the clubs they decorated one another
and set about writing history.
Parliaments were filled with pomp.
Then they divided up
the land, the law,
the best streets, air,
the University, shoes.

Their extraordinary initiative
was the State erected in this
form, the rigid imposture.
It was debated, as usual,
with solemnity and banquets,
first in agricultural circles,
with the military and lawyers.
And the supreme Law was finally
taken to Congress—the famous,
respected, untouchable
Funnel Law.
*   It was passed*
For the rich, square meals.
Garbage for the poor.
Money for the rich.
For the poor, work.
For the rich, mansions.

Hovels for the poor.
Exemptions for the robber baron.
Jail for the man who steals a loaf.
Paris, Paris for the dandies.
The poor to the mines, the desert.

Mr. Rodriguez de la Crota
spoke in the Senate with a mellifluous
elegant voice.
*   "This law, at long last, establishes*
the obligatory hierarchy
and above all the principles
of Christianity.
*   It was*
necessary as water.
Only the communists, conceived
in hell, as you're well aware,
could object to the Funnel
code, sagacious and severe.
But this Asiatic opposition,
proceeding from subman,
is easy to suppress: to jail with
them all, to the concentration camp,
and that way the distinguished
gentlemen and the obliging
Radical Party lackeys
will stand alone."

There was a round of applause
from the aristocratic benches:
what eloquence, how spiritual,
what a philosopher, what a luminary!
And everyone ran off to fill
his pockets in his business,

one monopolizing milk,
another racketeering in wire,
another stealing in sugar,
and all boisterously proclaiming
themselves patriots, with a monopoly
on patriotism, also accounted for
in the Funnel Law.

ELECTION IN CHIMBARONGO

In Chimbarongo, Chile, long ago
I went to a senatorial election.
I saw how the pillars
of society were elected.
At eleven in the morning
ox carts crammed with sharecroppers
arrived from the country.
It was winter.Wet,
dirty, hungry, barefoot,
the serfs from Chimborongo
climb down from the ox carts.
Grim, sunburnt, tattered,
they're packed together, led
ballots in hand,
marshalled in a bunch
to draw their pay and,
herded like horses,
they're led back
to the ox carts again.

   Then
they're thrown meat and wine
until they're left brutally
debauched and forgotten.

Later I heard the speech
of the senator thus elected:
"We, Christian patriots,
we, defenders of the order,
we, children of the spirit."
And his belly trembled,
his voice of a besotted cow
that seemed to sway
like a mammoth's trunk
in the sinister caverns
of howling prehistory.

When he finished, the room was silent. Then everyone stood up and applauded as he sat down quietly next to Matilde.

Harold and I were honored to be the only people invited back to the Nerudas' hotel room. There, waiting for us, was a delicious dinner of pâté and duck, prepared by the hotel's restaurant. Neruda opened a bottle of vintage red wine, and we all sat down at a small table to eat together.

Matilde began to complain, lovingly, "Pablo's greatest vice is that he loves good food. I think that must come from the time when he was poor and had nothing to eat. Now the doctor says he has gout and he's supposed to drink mineral water only and eat vegetables, but what can I do? I can't deny Pablo anything, because he is Pablo." She laughed. Harold was so busy already feasting that he had nothing to say. But in the middle of the delicious meal, Pablo stopped and talked seriously to me.

"Linda—I call you Linda because you are so young and beautiful and *Linda* means 'beautiful' in Spanish," he began. "Linda, I need the help of an American poet whom I can trust."

"You can trust me with anything," I said.

116

"One day. I do not know when. Perhaps in five years. Perhaps in seven. Perhaps ten. There will be a change of government in my country. In 1945 I was elected senator in Chile. I campaigned for a man who I thought would be good for the country, Gabriel González Videla. Even to say his name now makes me choke. Makes me spit blood. When he won the presidency, he backed away from all his promises and outlawed the communists. I wrote an open letter to him, accusing him of betrayal. An order for my arrest was immediately issued on the grounds of treason and contempt, when it was I who had traveled all over the country on his behalf to get him elected. I went into hiding, pursued by the police. I was then writing *Canto General* feverishly. My escape on horseback through the Andes is a story of intrigue which is known by many and which I will tell you about some other time, Sandra."

"The Chilean government even released news of his death," Matilde broke in.

"You're the great hero poet," Harold threw in, finished with his food and now totally mesmerized, as was I, by Pablo's remarks.

Pablo continued. "In 1959, last year, still in my role as itinerant poet, I was named the Chilean ambassador to Mexico, and I will be working for the rest of my life to get rid of the appalling atrocities committed in my country. At the same time, I am writing poetry, which is a way of trying to not only write history but to look with fresh eyes at the humblest elements of reality, because, Sandra, after all, a poet does not just write about revolution. A poet must write about his own legs, a cup, a broom, and of course must write about his or her own life, and about love. I have no wish to leave my planet; I do not care about going to the moon. But I care about a just and kind and compassionate man running for president of my country and being elected by the people. Such a man is my old friend since childhood, Dr. Salvador Allende. When this happens, it will be a time of hope, and then I want to invite you as my guest to come to my country, to meet everyone in my country from the very rich to the poor. I want you to meet our poets, to listen to the music of Violeta Parra, to be my guest at Isla Negra, and most of all to interview Dr. Allende and go back to your own country and tell the truth about what a great man he is. I know you will not betray me. And when that day comes, you will tell the world who this man is and who *we* are. That is what I want you to do. Until then, we will always be in touch. While we are here in Paris, we can visit, and then we will write and call each other. You will read me your new poems and I will read you mine. And one day I will send for you."

I was silent, and then I told him that I would be honored to do what he asked. The evening ended with listening to a recording of the songs of the Chilean poet and songwriter Violeta Parra, and then we all embraced, and Harold and I left.

"Wow. Man, that was heavy," Harold said when we were driving home. "I thought the movie would be a bummer, but it was fantastic. And the poems? I think they are just as moving in English as they are in Spanish. I was just sorry he didn't read the one about the United Fruit Company."

"So was I, but I don't think he wanted to inflame the American consul general and people from our embassy."

"But man, when he had us back at his hotel pad, and he served us this great dinner—I mean, that was really fine, fine dining—his asking you to come to visit him one day in Chile and write about this dude Salvador Allende, that was a *trip*. Whenever that's gonna be, maybe not for a while, but when it happens, man, I hope you'll let me come with you. I speak perfect Spanish. And I promise not to run after any queers, just stay with you. What a great trip that's gonna be. Maybe we can even sneak away to Easter Island and see those huge stone face carvings that look like *New Yorker* cartoons. Nobody knows who made them; they may have been dropped from Mars."

"We'll see," I said. My mind was filled with annunciations, invitations, and fatigue. It had been a long, exciting day.

The next morning also dawned beautiful and sunny. My new sidekick—bushy-eyebrowed Harold—and I decided to treat ourselves, on my money of course, to croissants and hot chocolate at the Café Deux Magots. Who did we run into? None other than the extraordinary and bohemian couple Alain Jouffroy and Manina. Manina, like Anaïs Nin, had created a legend out of her own persona. She always wore costumes—very high heels, fishnet stockings to show off her legs, bright pink dresses, and her own chunky silver jewelry. With her mop of black hair, her huge blue incandescent eyes, her perfect small nose, and her white teeth set off by very pink lipstick, she was as glamorous as any movie star. The fact that she was at least twenty years older than her lover, Jouffroy, who was in his late twenties, made no difference. They were the royalty of the avant-garde Paris art scene, with Alain having the power of the pen through a leading arts magazine to either make or break artists.

Sitting next to Alain was his buddy Jean-Jacques Lebel, whom I had met briefly at the bookstore signing. He gave me a big smile and gallantly pulled out one of the wicker chairs for me to sit on. The conversation was centered on the Machu Picchu film that Harold and I had seen the evening before.

Harold, tooting his own horn, took full credit for our being invited, making everyone at the table envious of the fact that *they* had not received an invitation to the exclusive and exemplary event where Pablo had read his poetry. Manina and Alain, like most of the painters, critics, poets, and filmmakers on the Left Bank, were liberals, and Neruda was a hero.

"His theme was betrayal," Harold said as everyone sat quietly, listening to him in awe. Harold loved being the center of attention.

"We were all being betrayed by crumbling European empires," Alain said with his thick French accent.

We sat together in camaraderie until Lebel jumped up and said, "I'm going to take Sandra on a tour of the art galleries." He asked me, "Would you like to spend the day with me?"

"Thank you! I've been so busy being the little wife in the concert world, I haven't gone to any galleries and have no idea really of the new art scene. I've seen a blue Yves Klein painting in the apartment of René and Madame Leibowitz, but that's about it."

"I can't stand Leibowitz," Jouffroy threw in. "What a phony. His discordant music is like going to a Chinese New Year celebration."

"Well, he's living and leading an orchestra in Switzerland now," I added, wanting to drop the subject.

"Come on," said Jean-Jacques, picking up the check for everyone. And he and I were off.

Walking with Lebel, I felt young and carefree. I remembered that I was a girl, not an old woman. I hadn't realized until *that moment* what being with much older people all the time had done to me. It had robbed me of my youth, of my get-up-and-go, of my enthusiasm for running around and being untroubled. Shomsky was thirty-eight, and most of his musical fans and colleagues were even older. And now here I was with a gorgeous young man who seemed to be in his late teens, and I was feeling like a teenager myself.

We walked hand in hand along the Seine, passing flea markets, antique stalls, vegetable markets, the hurly-burly of Paris on a bright summer day.

"The art world is exploding," Lebel said. "Have you ever been to any artist's studios?"

"Only one. The studio of Mané-Katz, when my father and his girlfriend were visiting Shomsky and me, and I was trying to get my father to buy one of his paintings."

"Mané-Katz? Is he still alive?"

"Yes," I said. "He's probably in his sixties."

"His paintings are shit. He's a second-rate Chagall. But Chagall, at least, had a sense of humor. Mané-Katz should be hung in funeral parlors. His work is dead. I'll show you some artists that really cook."

We walked on the Rue Bonaparte. There was an exhibit of Victor Brauner, the surrealist painter. His work was colorful, and I loved it. I felt so alive looking at his paintings.

The next gallery was a surprise to me. They were showing an exhibition of Jean-Jacques's paintings and collages. When we walked in, I saw a wonderful collage called *André Breton et Guillaume Apollinaire,* which showed Breton as a wolf and Apollinaire as a person in profile with a musician inside his head. It was breathtakingly surrealistic and original. I loved it. Another was a painting called *Le Soleil et la Substance,* which looked like an explosion of shells and fruit in dazzling colors of orange and red and brown.

"You see that?" he asked, pointing to a part of the painting that looked like a shell. "That's a vagina," he said, laughing. He walked me over to another huge painting titled *Jeune Ocean.* It was all swirls of colors and forms. "I exhibited that in Florence," he said. There was a red dot next to it, which meant it had been sold.

My favorite of all was a surrealist collage titled, in English, *A Few Good Screws.* It had been created in 1958. There was a black and white photograph of a woman sleeping. At the bottom was a hand, in color, with painted red nails. Around the woman's head were photographs of actual screws. It was erotic, mysterious, and dream-like. "It's fabulous," I said.

Jean-Jacques led me to the back of the gallery to see one of his huge, unsold "masterpieces." I had to agree that it was very powerful. Titled *Corps Mémorable,* it was a painted kaleidoscope of figures and faces, wings and blood. Next to it was another enormous, impressionistic work, part collage, part painting: *Portrait of Solitude.* The background—inserted into the painting, as if it were a mirror—was influenced by Jackson Pollock's drip-painting technique. There were photographs of a woman's face and of nude bodies. The woman's face, shockingly, resembled my own.

Jean-Jacques saw my reaction. He laughed. "You see? I met you in a dream long before I ever met you in reality." I enjoyed his laughter, which was like the cackle of a hen about to sit on her eggs. It was a long *ha-ha-ha-ha-ha,* and it was catching, so I began laughing too.

I realized, *Oh my God, I'm actually laughing. I am actually happy.* I had lived in a penitentiary of misery and had not been happy since the moment I had been sucked into the life of Shomsky by some fatal act of the gods. I had lived like a miserable prisoner with Shomsky at 36 Rue de Lille. I had existed and survived, but I had never been happy. And now I was. From that moment, I knew that I loved Jean-Jacques Lebel and always would.

We walked into the street, and Jean-Jacques gave me a childish smooch on the cheek. I turned my head a little bit, and it turned into a passionate kiss. I could feel his tongue in my mouth and taste his saliva, and it was as if the mercury of happiness went up another degree as we kissed on the street like new lovers. We broke away from the kiss, and Jean-Jacques behaved as if nothing had happened. He was cool. He had no idea how excited and truly happy I was. Poof. Magic. Sadness gone.

"Hey, I have a great idea," Jean-Jacques said. He was like a child when he got excited. I could tell he was very pleased that I appreciated his artwork. "Let's go to the studio of Tinguely."

"Who is that?"

"My God, you live in a world that is totally uninformed about the art scene. He's a Swiss sculptor who invented sculptures that are like machines and self-destruct. They move and dance almost like clocks. They even speak."

"How fascinating."

"And he's a really great guy. He works in a studio that's located in the most unique and secretive part of Paris. The Impasse de Vincennes. There are several sculpture studios there. The American sculptor James Metcalf has a studio there. It's where Brâncuși used to work. Tinguely is a fanatic workaholic, so he's always there creating. Let's go."

The Impasse de Vincennes was a series of about six sculpture studios that were originally large houses set together in a row. Tinguely welcomed us into his huge studio, which was filled with enormous steel shapes that looked to me like metal trees. They were attached to wires and plugged into an electrical outlet in the wall. He turned one sculpture on, and it started slowly gyrating. It was a movable sculpture that not only had density and a certain form and material, but that also moved.

"Isn't this beautiful?" Tinguely said about his own work. The sculptures were tick-tocking like huge clocks as they waved their arms and jerked around. I remembered dancing in the ballet *Coppélia* when I was at Cherry Lawn. I danced the role of the doll Coppélia; the master doll maker was named Dr. Coppélius. Now here was Dr. Coppélius as a sculpture.

We sat around a coffee table and shared a bottle of wine and some cheese while the sculptures moved in rhythm around us.

"So how's the Anti-Process going?" Tinguely asked Jean-Jacques.

"It's fabulous. Everyone is coming. The Death Barge"—
Jean-Jacques's project to float protesting artists down the
Venice canals in black-draped barges—"is going to be
written about all over the world. History every moment. Art
through media."

"He's quite the provocateur, your friend," Tinguely said.
"While I create with steel, he creates with manifestations,
readings, happenings, demonstrations, as well as with collages
and paintings. He's probably the most important artist here
on the scene in Paris. A combination between Castro and
Cézanne."

Jean-Jacques said, "One day my whole idea is that artists
who change the world will be understood. I plan to go to
America, Italy, Germany, and China and demonstrate that art
is not just meant for beauty. Art is meant to create strikes. It's
not just perfume. It's also a brutality. Right now I'm planning
a free-expression workshop. I am not just setting up international art shows and manifestations in Europe and the U.S.
Oh, no. My controversial happenings will occur on the streets,
in the galleries, and even in insane asylums."

"What if painting follows the cinema and abandons
its spiritual aims and becomes just another industry?"
Tinguely asked.

Jean-Jacques answered with rage. "In Tokyo, Milan,
Paris, and New York, this seems to be the present trend: art
is more and more being treated like merchandise, manufac-
tured and consumed, bought and sold, counted in inventory
just like any other product. And the artist more and more
is considered—and considers himself—a mere employee of
the cultural industry."

Tinguely punctuated the conversation with his own anger,
speaking articulately but with a slight Swiss accent. I couldn't
help but notice that he was extremely handsome, with his dark
hair, dark eyes, and articulate upper-class hands. "This rather

new sociological relationship between the creator and society is not yet fully appraised. In fact, the age-old question of 'What is art?' is even harder now to answer than ever."

"Tinguely, you are so right," Lebel said. He grew very animated as he rose to the task of spewing out his complaints about the art world. "All over the world, critics, museum curators, artists are all busy as bees passionately buzzing around the questions of where the boundaries between high art and kitsch, the true and the phony, actually lie. Yet the very existence of such boundaries is sometimes denied. Can one forget that only a generation ago, Brâncuși's sculpture was allowed freely into the United States by a customs official precisely because it *wasn't* art? My friend Henry Geldzahler, of New York's Metropolitan Museum, declared at the Museum of Modern Art's symposium on pop art, 'I have heard it said that pop art is not art'—and this by a museum curator! My feeling is that it is the artist who defines the limits of art, not the curator or the critic."

"And this is not all," said Tinguely, now drinking another glass of red wine and looking relaxed. "And this is not all the bullshit that exists in the art world. We must ask: can we artists who actually rock the foundation of culture, and in some cases of society itself, rightfully *expect* to be understood, recognized, or even tolerated without a fight?"

"This is exactly the point of my workshop on free expression," Jean-Jacques said to Tinguely, "and I want you to take part in it. We have decided to fit into one of our festivals as many other artistic expressions as we can. We have decided to ignore culture's absurd classifications and to unite in one festival with as many artists' experiences as possible. We're going to open with a jazz festival, a poetry festival, and then there will be a series of happenings, dream sequences staged in reality. There will even be a movie by Man Ray and a great new documentary on Marcel Duchamp."

"I'll be there," Tinguely said.

"Count me in too," I said, feeling passionate about the new power of art to change lives.

The sculptor looked at his watch. He threw on a dark blue cashmere scarf, even though it was very warm, and said he had to leave for an appointment.

"You're welcome to stay here," he said cordially to Jean-Jacques, "with your charming American friend, and finish the bottle of wine."

"Super," Jean-Jacques replied.

It was now late afternoon. Jean-Jacques took me in his arms and kissed me with a passion I had never experienced. Slowly we took off our clothes. We made love, and I felt as if we were two nebulae in the sky, exploding. It was as if the nebulae were glowing pink and blue. We were not so much making love as igniting each other. Afterward we drank a glass of wine.

"You're coming to Venice with me," Jean-Jacques said.

That night, when I returned to my apartment, I looked in the mailbox and there was no letter from Shomsky. When I entered my house, there was little Harold waiting for me. He threw down the book he was reading and jumped off my bed, where he had made himself at home.

"What happened?" he asked.

"We went gallery hopping, and it was wonderful. And then we visited the sculpture studio of Tinguely."

"Did you make love?" Harold asked, eager for details.

"I feel guilty about it. But we did."

"Guilty? Why should you feel guilty? Sex is the greatest thing in the world. The world doesn't run on time. Mutual orgasms are what everyone in the world is looking for. The mutual explosion. *That* throughout history is what every person looked for. The power ends in sex. Sex is the power. Sex is everything. If you found great sex, never let go of it. Sandra, do you understand what I'm telling you? The secret of the universe? If you and Lebel hit it off sexually, you should drop Shomsky in a minute and go and be with him. People kill for great sex. What did it feel like?"

"As if I was suddenly me. I always feel light years away from who I am. Suddenly I was nebulae in the sky. I felt born."

"You better thank God you found this guy," Harold said wisely. "This is going to change your life."

"He wants me to go to Venice."

"To the Anti-Process?"

"Yes."

"Then go. It will be a glorious circus. A fabulous art circus. You'll never forget it as long as you live."

"Harold, I suddenly feel tired. Do you mind if I go to sleep?"

"It's your house. Go ahead. I'll go upstairs and read."

I undressed and got under the cool white sheets. As I lay in bed, scenes of my life with Shomsky started running through my head like a film. So many scenes. Memories of the limitations of my marriage.

I woke up. Was it all a bad dream? I remembered looking for apartments in Paris. Up stairs and down stairs. Leaks and cold water. A phone call from my father: "My daughter shouldn't be running around with a bunch of no-good artists."

Instead, I rented a car without a hood and drove somewhere in the country—Normandy—to be myself, whoever she was. I grew and grew. Suddenly I woke up breathing through the gills. I had turned into a sea maiden and set out for the dangerous place under the water. There I saw my father: "You have come home," he said to me.

I stood there. I was drowning in a memory of how I was not allowed to have a life of my own by my jealous genius husband.

Another memory filtered through my mind before sleep. Marcel Marceau often came to visit us in our apartment at 36 Rue de Lille. He was an old friend of Shomsky's, and I looked forward to his visits because he was the only person in Shomsky's circle, besides Cocteau, who ever paid the slightest attention to me. Marceau's real last name was Mangel. He was Jewish and had grown up in Strasbourg, and he and his brother had been part of the Resistance during the war. Marceau had been entranced in his childhood by theatre troupes that performed *commedia dell'arte,* and after the war he had sought out Étienne Decroux, the master of classical mime, to be his teacher. Single-handedly Marceau had changed the face of theater by returning the art of mime to its pristine form.

When Marcel came to visit us, he loved to talk. He spoke in articulate French and sometimes English, creating his ideas not only verbally but also with his magnificent hands, which helped shape his ideas as they flew through the air like two white birds. It turned out that Marceau also loved to paint— as did I—and when he saw my watercolors lying on a table, we were drawn closer by our mutual love of painting. One afternoon he suggested to Shomsky that Shomsky *let me* come study at the school of mime Marceau had founded at his theater in Paris, where he performed with his company. When he learned that I had been an actress—I had performed at the Circle in the Square Theatre, in New York—he thought that I would be an excellent addition to his small class.

Shomsky, of course, didn't like the idea at all. But Marcel persisted and charmed him. It was difficult for Shomsky to refuse Marcel anything—they were great pals—and Shomsky finally said yes. Marceau had just acted out one of his new mimodramas—mime plays—in our drawing room. It was based on Gogol's *Le Manteau,* and Marcel of course played all the parts for us. It was thrilling. Shomsky was in a good mood that day, and it was settled: I could go once a week and study with Marceau. Shomsky decided to give me "permission."

Suddenly, freedom was mine. On Thursdays, I ran out of our apartment, forgetting chores and leaving Shomsky to practice or speak on the phone, and arrived on the steps of the Ambigu Theatre. To enter the world of velvet seats and lights and a proscenium stage was a reprieve for me. Marceau taught me the craft of illusion—of growing taller and shrinking. He taught me balance and how to mime being on a tightrope and throwing imaginary objects like balls. He was an inspiring teacher. He showed me how to physicalize characters and how to get the "instrument" of my body in shape. I had watched him create David and Goliath on stage, and it was in his classes that I saw how the body can expand like a bellows, or contract. I learned how to give mime characters flesh, blood, and inner life. In an odd way, I was learning not only to be a mime, but also how to *write.*

One night, Shomsky came home from a concert after I had been at a mime class. I was feeling jubilant, as if I had touched the center of my mind and body. As students, we were allowed to see the performances without paying, and I had gone to a matinee of Marcel's show in which he portrayed the character of Bip, his own Chaplinesque character. I was inspired by watching the musicality of his work. He was a one-man *commedia dell'arte* vaudeville act and was able to evoke all the human emotions.

"I love this class," I confided to Shomsky. I could hardly wait for Thursdays to arrive.

"I'm sorry, we're leaving for Portugal. I told Marcel you're no longer able to study with him."

I watched Shomsky carefully. He was packing a large suitcase.

"You told *him?* Why didn't you let *me* tell him?"

"What difference does it make?"

I realized that my Thursdays of freedom were gone.

I remembered all this after Shomsky left for Cuba. He would take away anything from me that I loved. He wanted to use my youth and energy for himself.

All this had been part of my old life. My life with Shomsky. Now my new life had begun.

5.

Jean-Jacques, Enfant Terrible

Like a phoenix, I awoke from my dreams and bad memories. I was young and depressed. Who was I really?

As I sat in my bed thinking about the mess of my life, I saw my life as a ball of thread that was unwinding in the labyrinth of Paris. Was Jean-Jacques the minotaur who would come looking for me? My life seemed absurd, like an Ionesco play. My childhood at Cherry Lawn had made me want to escape the bourgeois, meaningless existence that my parents had carved out for themselves from the lard of their lives. They had both been children of Jewish immigrants—Ashkenazi Jews from Russia—who had grown up during the Depression worshipping the idol of success. They had sent me away to be raised in an institution that had eventually crippled me because it had made me "fantasize" about the beauty of a home and a normal life. In that fantasy I had run off with Shomsky, whom I worshipped as a hero simply because he was a fiddler and not a peddler. He was not a salesman like my father or an ambulance chaser like my mother's professional-man second husband, whom I looked at with critical eyes because he never showed me any affection. (It took many years before I realized that my stepfather was someone who loved me, before I could see his good points and accept them both.) I thought how stupid it was that I had wanted someone to take care of me but instead had wound up being the caretaker.

What was I to Shomsky? Nothing but a glorified nurse. I thought if I made myself his little helper, he would love me. My mother used little expressions that summed up the meaning of life in a corny sort of Hallmark-card way—for example, to have a friend, you have to *be* a friend. Well, she was right and yet wrong. I had been Shomsky's friend, but he had never returned the favor. There was now nothing friendly about him. I was his mistress, his wife, his cook, his manager, and all I had to show for my efforts of being giving and kind and considerate was that he had sucked me into the vacuum-cleaner bag of his own age, of his selfishness, of his egomaniacal obsession with fame. Why hadn't I been a better friend to myself and gotten my own fame?

He was drunk on his own needs. And like a drunk, he had alcoholic behavior, even though he wasn't an alcoholic. He was a baby. I had read somewhere that Vladimir Horowitz demanded of his wife, Wanda, that she take care of her little genius. But Wanda, I suspected, got off on being Mrs. Horowitz in the skating rink of the arts, where she could glide behind her husband as he did his musical turns and jumps, because she knew she would never be a skater herself. She would never be a genius. She liked living through another person. I did not. Deep in my heart, I was certain that I could be an artist too.

I didn't want to be Madame Shomsky all the time. I wanted my own career as a poet. Now that Harold Norse had introduced me to Pablo Neruda, the world's greatest poet as far as I was concerned, and he had encouraged me and read my work out loud to his wife, saying, "This is beautiful, so beautiful" over and over again, I was beginning to believe it. If Anaïs Nin was willing to publish my book of poems with her own money and the money of the English poet Lawrence Durrell, then it was important that I run away from my job of babysitter to a would-be star and find the inner peace that came with having control of my life.

I wanted to have the courage to find a solitary life that would allow my juices to flow in poetry. But having clung to the raft of marriage with Shomsky, I was frightened of being afloat in the huge ocean of life by myself. To be a loner requires courage and a sense of inner peace. The ability to love your inner labyrinth. I wasn't cut out to be a yogi, to breathe deeply and find my inner self. I had spent my whole life surrounded by thousands of people: first the gaggle of friends I had cultivated in boarding school, where being popular meant survival. Then at Bennington I had clung to my professors and to my so-called mentor, James T. Farrell, who was my literary daddy. I had also clung to all the girlfriends whom I talked to constantly on the phone, exchanging secrets and confidences and depending on them emotionally.

Shomsky was, above all, a people person. Like his good friend the conductor Leonard Bernstein, he was a huggy-kissy kind of "Dahling, I love you" person and a professional courtier who made the music world his court. There wasn't one evening when he and I were alone together. I never had the life of solitude that I needed because our life was all about him and his needs, not about mine. I hadn't dated until I met Shomsky because I didn't want superficial and disturbing experiments with sexuality and intimacy to distract my focus from my work. With my writing, I had been like a boxer: I led with my jaw, I boxed against the shadows of other poets, trying to make myself a winner. Then I had given all that up. Now Shomsky was the boxer. I was merely a coach sitting on the sidelines. But were the sidelines where I wanted to be?

How did I stop being a trainer and start boxing again? With what money? With what food? Where was I to live? Could I be a boxer of poetry in the ring of my father's penthouse? Of course not. Living with Sidney would mean having to play the role of the nice Jewish girl doing what my father wanted. How could I find independence? The adventure of a free life?

What I really wanted was to have my own apartment.

I wanted to be on my own again, without a man, the way I had once been at Bennington. I knew that relationships, especially sexual relationships, were the death of the woman artist. I couldn't be wife, mother, maid, manager, and mistress and still be left alone to think. But I knew that my conventional father with all his money as bribe material would never send me an allowance to just sit and write poetry. It was bad enough that I was yoked to a man he couldn't stand. He would never shell out the bucks for me to be independent. He felt he owned me. He wanted me to take care of him. And Shomsky wanted a caregiver also. Without some kind of job, I couldn't be independent.

The problem was, I didn't have a green card to work in Paris. I would have to go back to America and find some sort of job. Give up the crucifix of marriage. And sweat it out alone. But could I do that? Why was I so weak? So needy? So unsure of my own powers?

As always, I consoled myself by meeting Peggy Peterson at the Deux Magots and talking not about Shomsky but about the present. I was hoping that Jean-Jacques would help me discover who I really was.

"Well," I said to Peggy, "Shomsky is gone."

"Anyone else in your life?" she asked. She knew that

Shomsky and I had a dead marriage, and that I was angry that he had dumped me to go off to Cuba.

"There is someone I just met," I confided. *Now* she was interested. Peggy lived vicariously through everyone else's love affairs. She was a nosy angel who loved gossip.

"Who?"

"You won't mention it to anyone?"

"Of course not."

"You promise."

"I swear."

"Well, nothing has happened yet in the Biblical sense," I lied. That was an old Bennington College expression. I didn't want to admit I'd had fantastic sex with this young-seeming man I had just met.

"Tell me. I'm dying to know," she said.

I told her that I was in love with a famous media star who seemed to be about eighteen. I felt nauseous and guilty, but glad to get the truth out of my stomach. "Does the name Jean-Jacques Lebel mean anything to you?" I asked.

She stared at me in disbelief. "Do you really mean the young revolutionary who is in all the papers? Lebel the troublemaker, the obnoxious young headline-grabbing surrealist painter? Like the nihilist Picabia?" She told me that when Dadaism and surrealism were being born in Zurich in 1916 at the Cabaret Voltaire, Jean-Jacques Lebel's father had been there as an onlooker journalist, chronicling it all so the Dadaists could have an instant art legacy. Cabaret Voltaire was established by Hugo Ball—along with his friends and cofounders Tristan Tzara, Hans Arp, Marcel Janco, and Richard Huelsenbeck—as a venue for a miniature variety show. All the Dadaists had left their countries as a result of World War I. Ball and Huelsenbeck came from Germany, Tzara and Janco from Romania, Hans Arp from France. "They agreed that the war had been contrived by the various governments for the most outrageously autocratic, disgusting, and materialistic reasons," Peggy said. "Lebel's father, who was then in his teens, wrote down the ravings of the Dadaists, who saw all the French politicians as flat-headed and vile. Out of that cabaret came the energies for the great international artistic movements. The older Lebel recounted it all and became famous." She paused. "And Jean-Jacques has picked up where those lunatics left off."

I listened to Peggy, fascinated. She was a dispenser of cultural gossip and seemed to know everything about artistic politics. Art history had been her major at Radcliffe, and it was rumored that her grandmother had been a follower of Gertrude Stein. When it came to art history, she had the memory of an elephant.

"My God, how fabulous," I said.

"Well, here's the scoop," Peggy continued, drinking now, as easily as any alcoholic, which I suspected she was, a double Pernod on the rocks. "When the Nazis came to power, the Lebels fled Paris for the United States. Jean-Jacques would have been a little boy at this time. He was an enfant terrible who was dandled on the knee by his father's good friend Marcel Duchamp. Max Ernst was his godfather. Jean-Jacques's father read manifestos to him at night. He didn't read about the Three Little Bears; he read literature which taught him that art and literature were made to have a gun in their hand. Jean-Jacques's dream as a little boy, I'm sure, was to be a robber baron of the pen. He was taught by the surrealists and the Dadaists, who were exiles and visited his parents' apartment, that to be a philosopher in a garret or a classroom was thoroughly obsolete—but so was the professional artist, the *littérateur,* the society wit, the man who could be moved in any way by intellectual accomplishment, but who was meaningless in the Dadaist worldview. The baby Dadaist, Jean-Jacques learned as a boy, was to be the opposite of the bourgeois child. I remember reading in one of Robert Lebel's books, the one he wrote before he wrote on the the life of Picabia, 'The Dadaist looks forward to the day, fully aware that a flower pot may fall on his head. He is naïve, he loves the noises of the Métro, he likes to hang around Cooks Travel Bureau and knows the practices of the angel makers who behind closely drawn curtains dry out foetuses on blotting paper in order to grind them up and sell them as ersatz coffee.'"

"Tell me more," I said. I was beginning to realize that Peggy was not just an American girl I had met on the bus but an Eiffel Tower of information about Dadaism and surrealism.

She continued. Lebel saw that in Tzara's hands Dadaism had achieved great triumphs. The Dadaists wrote books and published manifestos that were circulated all over Europe before World War II. They put on shows to which thousands of curious people came. Soon the radical world press adopted the Dada movement in art. The founders of Dada knew above all how to set the big rotary presses of the media in motion. Dada was never discussed in the École de France or in the books of the fashionable psychoanalysts. But it became regarded as a ridiculous product of modern artistic madness. Tzara and Ball founded an art gallery, the Galerie Dada, which exhibited futuristic pictures. It ridiculed the art business at literary teas, lectures, and artistic events.

Peggy continued, "Soon, Hitler's grotesque platform of insanity conquered the world, and they dispersed. Everyone went underground. In America, Jean-Jacques grew up listening to the conversations of the Dadaists in his parents' living room and learned to ignore 'art for art's sake.' He became a fanatic of the Dada aesthetic and the power of the artist/revolutionary to stand up to the bourgeois aesthetics of Western Europe and America and overthrow them. In the 1950s, when he returned with his parents to France, he was still a child of sixteen, but a child with revolution on his mind. Like the young Rimbaud, he already wrote like an angel, but not poetry: he wrote manifestos and found his life's calling in waging war against the hypocrites of society. His goal in life, his bridge to eternity, was and is to create revolution, to organize students against their parents and the bourgeois society they are forced into, and to remind students that it is their obligation to turn against the monarchy of the art dealers and publishers who, he believes, pathologically deform society."

I continued listening with eager anticipation for what she would say next.

"Jean-Jacques has sworn in the press to do all this with a sense of Dadaist absurdity. Not for him, communist social realism. No. Lebel's no communist. Dada is his weapon, the guerrilla warfare of political happenings that capture the imagination of the press and their millions of readers. The publishers and the tabloids that circulate action photographs and details of Lebel's dozens of events against society become his political paintbrush and political tool. His logo of political awareness is *Merz,* which is a word invented by the German Dadaist Kurt Schwitters, who influenced Picabia. And therefore Jean-Jacques Lebel wants to topple society." She paused again.

"Merz? I love it." I exploded. I was beginning to fall even more in love with Jean-Jacques because I too was a secret revolutionary, rebelling against the academic poetry I had learned at Bennington and the materialistic values of my parents and so-called peers back in America. Most of my Bennington friends were now conventional and boring. With Shomsky, I thought I had run away to a radical world of classical music and beauty, only to find out what a phony social climber he really was. As I sat in the café with Peggy, I thought what a mistake my marriage was. Shomsky had no ideals or beliefs. He was a genius for hire. He was engaged in playing his violin at the celebration of Castro's revolution of Cuba Libre, but I knew he could just as easily be engaged to play at the Rothschild bar mitzvah or at the salon for all the corporate panhandlers and scumbag bankers, and to French kiss the establishment who pretended to like classical music.

Unlike my new crowd of friends, Shomsky played the fiddle when the money was right. I had never adjusted to the elements of his life, which were not about art at all, but about making money for the purpose of impressing people, especially the very rich, so he could shout, as a poor boy, that he was as good as they were. He may have seduced me by saying he loved my poetry and my mind, but once I had lived with him for a year or so, I realized that his love was meaningless. At first he had been my musical angel, my David with a lyre, my Orpheus. But he had killed my sexual desire for him with his lies, his narcissism, and his phony idealism.

Jean-Jacques Lebel radiated to me the creative energy of a bad-boy rebel that I immediately found so attractive. Seeming to be five years younger than I was (even though we were the same age), it was as though he came from another world of youth. I had studied at the progressive Cherry Lawn School and then at Bennington College, where my eyes had been opened to modern literature, modern dance, and labor problems (one of my favorite subjects). Then I had chosen not to work in the theater but to run off to Paris, which I believed to be the cultural capital of the world, only to find myself in the stifled bourgeois realm of classical music. But the musical world was actually feudal with its worship of managers like Hurok and of patrons of orchestras known as nobles. Theorists such as Shomsky in some way were still serfs dependent on noblesse oblige and on playing many concerts to make a living.

"Merz," Peggy continued, "stands for freedom from all fetters for the sake of artistic creation. It also means tolerance toward any artistically motivated limitation. Every artist must be allowed to make a picture out of nothing but blotting paper, for example. If you really want to understand this

Jean-Jacques," she said, "you should read Jacques Vaché, his letters to André Breton."

Peggy finished her Pernod. She had encouraged me in my liaison with René Leibowitz, which had turned out to be a disaster. And now she was *warning* me to stay away from Jean-Jacques Lebel. Yet as I talked with her, I realized that I could not help myself. Lebel had stirred feelings inside my body, sexual feelings, that I'd never felt for Leibowitz, or even for Shomsky, who had been my first great love. Lebel was not very tall, but his madman's curly blond hair, which coiled around his neck, his piercing blue eyes, and most of all his full lips attracted me. His bad-boy giggle, the trouble-making twinkle in his eyes, his antiestablishment rap, his youthful fingers all made me want to jump up from my chair at the Deux Magots and run away from Peggy and into his arms. I already knew he was going to be the next great love of my life. I knew it in the mysterious collage that exists between the belly and the heart and the lips of the vagina and the chambers of the brain, in the cellular messages that consign all these parts of a woman's body into a flight of sound which persists, like a beating drum, and cannot be ignored. The sexual lymphatic system, which drowns out the anvil and cochlea of reason and has a mind of its own, was already making me deaf to Peggy's warnings. The more she put down this youthful revolutionary, the more inter-ested I grew. I was born a poet, which meant I was born with a troublemaking bad-girl gene, and it was this gene that attracted me to Jean-Jacques Lebel.

Is it true that every poet loves a rebel? Or was it just true for me? As a "bad girl" and the black sheep or black shepherdess of the Hochman family, I was attracted to agitators and scoun-drels. Shomsky had pretended to be a scoundrel but turned out to be merely a musician with an outgoing, manic person-ality who in reality was pursuing wealth and the status quo.

"Be careful of Jean-Jacques," Peggy warned, and it was exactly her warning that made Jean-Jacques Lebel seem even more attractive. His eyes had a devilish twinkle, and the devil was more attractive to me now than my boring husband, who had bolted for Cuba and made the mistake of leaving me alone in Paris. I felt rejected and yet liberated. My anger at being left behind fueled my need to find somebody else to love me.

I nervously accepted Jean-Jacques's invitation to hear him speak on a soapbox in his effort to recruit artists in the sixth arrondissement to join his new rebellion against the Venice Biennale, the establishment art show. It involved art dealers from all over the world showing their painters in what amounted to an art trade fair. The prestige of the Venice Biennale was enormous, and the curly-haired rebel Lebel was determined to destroy it.

"I am against the established art dealers and the grotesque inconsistencies of the art world!" he screamed. His soapbox speech was turning into what would later be called in New York a "happening." Anarchistic followers of Jean-Jacques were marching around his platform dressed in skull masks and black shrouds, representing death. "Death to the establishment!" Jean-Jacques sang out his aria.

The mummers, like a chorus of skeletons, echoed his words. "Death to the establishment!" they cried.

"Artists are fabulists of the imagination. They create a legacy for civilization. They are not shoes meant to be peddled by the art dealers, who are less than shoe salesmen."

"No dealers, no shoehorns!" the chorus screamed.

Parisians on their way to work stopped to listen. Children with their mouths open in amazement watched the media show. Cameras from different newspapers flashed as the paparazzi, who had been tipped off to the event by the media-savvy Jean-Jacques, snapped away at history.

"This is a proclamation inspired by the proclamation of Dadaist disgust. Art is going to sleep for a new world to be born. Musicians, smash your instruments. Blind men, take the stage. Art needs an operation. In this stagnated society, art is a pretension warmed by the timidity of the urinary basin, the hysteria born in the studio. We are in search of the force that is not the sobriety of the middle class. We are in search of nothing. We affirm the vitality of every instant. The antiphilosophy of spontaneous acrobatics. Get ready for the action of the geysers of our blood. Get ready for the manifestos of the antiphilosopher, anti–art dealer."

I stood in the crowd and listened as Lebel's high-pitched scream continued.

"I'll set up a boarding school for pimps and poets. I am an idiot, a clown, a fakir. But I bring revolution, and I urge you to call your family on the telephone and piss in the hole reserved for art and sacred stupidities."

Now the cameras were really snapping, like fireflies in the afternoon. The crowd of a few dozen turned into hundreds.

"Tristan Tzara, take a good look at us. We are your children. Stop looking. Stop talking. Death to the dealers at the art scam of the Venice Biennale. Join us in change," Lebel shouted to the throng of listeners.

The skull-faced students in death drag passed out leaflets urging whoever had the courage to sign up to go to Venice from Paris and join the Death Barge of the Biennale. More students arrived, waving red flags with skulls on them.

When the happening was over and Jean-Jacques jumped down from his antihero pedestal to applause while the cameras snapped his picture, he ran toward me and embraced me. A dozen photographers, as well as a newsreel cameraman, stood in front of us, filming and snapping. I wondered if this guerrilla-theater event would reach America and my father, God forbid, at the movies. Would he see me in the newsreel? I hoped not. On the other hand, it was ironic that my husband was in Cuba playing his fiddle to celebrate the heroism of Che Guevara and Castro, but back in Paris were the beginnings of the student revolution, which Jean-Jacques told me would in a few years become a real civil war that would overthrow de Gaulle.

Jean-Jacques promised that one day he and his buddy Danny the Red would emerge as leaders on the ramparts of change and would build up a following that would land them on the government's "most wanted" list and on the covers of *Time* and *Newsweek* in America and the front pages of newspapers all over the world. "This is only the beginning," he said. "This revolution will be the mustard seed of a big revolution in Paris. But the mustard seed has to grow."

I was thrilled to be there. Jean-Jacques hugged me. "Thank you for joining me," he said as he kissed me on the lips. "Come, let's get out of here."

He pushed his way through the admiring, screaming throng of anarchist sympathizers and held my hand as I was squeezed by the mob in their attempts to touch and hug Lebel. He was a rock-star revolutionary, handsome, daring, and pushing the buttons of the crowd with his theatricality, humor, anger, and radical Dada rhetoric.

Soon we were at the Brasserie Lipp, where I had sat with Shomsky and his idiot mistress and ogled the existentialists. Now I was the guest of a new-age revolutionary, the Third Wave nihilist Jean-Jacques, who found the existentialists to be absurd and ridiculous old fogies. "Juliette Gréco is a slut without brains. Sartre and Camus were old men who fought like senile children over a revolution they never led."

I felt that René Leibowitz, wherever he was, was a generation removed from this youth who wasn't at all interested in atonal music or the philosophy of Hegel, and who was making his legacy getting rid of the status quo. I had gone from being besotted by (and then disillusioned with) a sensual old man, to being enamored of a raging youngster who was drunk with revolution. He reminded me of the rebellious Rimbaud, whom I had worshipped while at Bennington. The man I had married, Shomsky, seemed like an old man compared to the radical Lebel. At twenty-four I was secretly flattered that Lebel was attracted to me, a married woman (here I had to laugh at myself).

"How would you like to be the girlfriend of a revolutionary?" Lebel asked. I was stunned. "I have a big cock. Why don't I whip it out and show it to you again?"

I laughed nervously. *I'm so wrong for you,* I thought. I was a romantic who, despite the fact that I wanted to be a writer, was a secret bourgeois. I loved beautiful things. I wanted a lovely home. I was definitely not the beatnik he thought I was. To begin with, I had been spoiled by attending the most expensive schools and being given everything else money could buy. Even though I had run off with a penniless Israeli violinist and we lived in relative poverty, we were always surrounded by very rich people. They might like modern music, but they were stuffy in their ways and wealthy enough to imagine they were artistic when they were really dilettantes and connoisseurs. Shomsky's world was the world of artists who worshipped art; they were mostly in their forties and fifties and sixties, and I was considered the young, pretty Jewish girl from America. Even though I had not fallen into the fate of most of my friends, which was to get married to doctors and lawyers and begin a family, I still had not yet found myself.

Anaïs Nin, who was now my patron in a sense, had decided to publish me, which gave me status in the eyes of Jean-Jacques; but Anaïs Nin was a rebel with a banker husband, and she was more of an aesthete than a revolutionary. The Paris I had lived in until Shomsky took off for Cuba was the fashionable Paris of the avant-garde. I had gone almost every day with Shomsky to the *nouvelle cinéma* or the Cinémathèque to see films made by Polanski or Godard or Truffaut, daring young filmmakers who were Shomsky's friends and who admired him because he was a charismatic musical genius. I had gone to fun parties with Jean Moreau and Marguerite Duras and Alain Resnais, who were all part of the fashionable Parisian Left. With Shomsky I had driven to the home of the novelist Françoise Sagan in Normandy, had dined with Alain Deloin and the super-stars Jean-Paul Belmondo and Jacques Charrier and Brigitte Bardot. On concert tours, I had spent time with aging lovers of the violin and had moved in a world of musical salons with Virgil Thomson. Classical-music lovers with their passion for concert halls were nothing at all like this revolutionary.

"What do you do most of the time?" Jean-Jacques asked me.

"I hang out with my husband at concerts," I said.

"And does Shomsky make a living with his violin?" Lebel asked with a hug that made me feel that his affection was more important than his questions. I could feel his youth and energy and virility, and I could tell that this was all small talk so we could go to bed.

"No," I said.

"I dig being with a married woman," he said, and as I looked into the irises of his blue eyes, I felt frightened of the attraction I felt for him. He seemed to like me and mock me at the same time.

"I hate concerts," he said. "It's all a lot of crap. Revolution is the only thing worth living for. I'm leaving tomorrow for Venice. The Death Barge is a great media-grabbing idea. It's going to capture the imagination of every paper in the world."

"Tell me more about the Death Barge?" I asked, feeling like a fool. As if I should know what he was talking about.

145

"You wouldn't have heard about it in the snooty circles you spend your time in. It's the most exciting idea to hit the art world in two thousand years of bullshit. It's a barge I've rented with some of my friends from Milano. I have a friend, Mario Ventelli. I'm sure you've never heard of him. He's a Marxist, which I forgive him for because he's like so many Italian Marxists: a millionaire and interested in changing the system. He owns a gallery, and a lot of the artists he represents are joining us in the Anti-Process. It's against the process, if you will, of the Biennale, which shows art to be bought and hung in galleries and museums. Art is not a commodity and it's not wallpaper. The art dealers are pimps who take 35 percent of the artist's earnings, sometimes 50 percent, and they have no idea what art is about. We have a lot of radical artists such as Masson and Wifredo Lam—who's a Cuban genius, another Picasso—joining us. We have many of the stars of the French art world joining us too: Tinguely, Hiquily, and Niki de Saint Phalle, who's the star of the Jolas Gallery, the most surrealist gallery in New York. Every one avant-garde. Even writers. Too bad Camus is dead, but his mistress will be on the boat. A few students, a few poets. We will have placards and flags, and we'll chant, 'Death to the dealers.' So while all the art patrons are in Venice buying paintings, all the dealers are buying art, we will be letting them know that their time is over. I've made all the signs for the demonstration, and when they see us holding them up, they will know that the Biennale is a fake and art as we know it is dead. Revolution is coming. The dealers will soon be part of the past. And of course all the media will cover us because this will shock them. We may be political clowns the way the Dadaists were, but humor is a weapon against the bourgeois who take art so seriously. Humor is the most political tool there is. We will laugh our way up the canals."

I wanted to say something relevant so I wouldn't seem like some dumb, bourgeois young poet in a blue denim coat who had nothing to contribute to society other than poetry. I wasn't some Bennington bimbo. I didn't want him to think that I wasn't a revolutionary or wasn't hip enough to understand him. I didn't do drugs. I wasn't really promiscuous and had only slept with two men in my life, my husband and Leibowitz, and I suddenly felt like a square. What should I say?

"What do you think of the Algerian War?" I asked, trying to sound political.

"Are you kidding? What do I think? I think the Algerians should have their freedom, of course. I'm on the side of all the Algerians who want to get out of the colonial shithouse. In fact, I keep a gun under my pillow for self-defense. But I'm for revolution in Paris just as much as I am for Algerian revolutionaries. We are all comrades. I want to get rid of de Gaulle and the charnel house of the French establishment. Their time is over. But we won't use revolvers: we will use the bullets of manifestos and the media. You'll see. Danny le Red and I are going to lead a student revolution that will awaken the world, and we will be joined by thousands of French students. You wait and see. Our country is even more corrupt than yours. Look at what Eisenhower is doing in Vietnam; that's going to be the death of America. Wait, you'll see. One day the artists are going to lead the world. The sleeping dogs of China are going to wake up and bite the world. They have billions of workers, and one day they will take the best of communism, merge with the capitalist pigs, and emerge as the most important force in the world. Fifty years from now, everyone will be speaking Mandarin. But as for the Algerians, they will definitely triumph. Once they learn how to organize their students they will triumph and be free."

"Do you know how to use a gun?" I asked.

"Why?"

"Because my husband, Shomsky, and I were hiding a nephew of the painter Masson, and after he was arrested he left his gun behind. His last words to me as they led him away were 'Now that I'm arrested, I'm no longer afraid of being arrested.'" I paused. "He gave me his gun."

"That's all bullshit. He shouldn't have been a lone fugitive. Besides, the war of the future won't just be a war of terrorists. It will be a war that media attention and technology use to influence minds."

"Then you don't want the gun?" I said meekly.

"No. My revolution is without guns. I want to leave here and make love to you. My cock is my gun," Jean-Jacques said arrogantly.

"You mean your weapon of destruction?" I asked.

"No, my weapon of seduction," he laughed.

He called for the check. I was having my first day of education in the Jean-Jacques Lebel school of revolution.

To show off my knowledge I replied, "I heard that Renoir said, 'I paint with my penis.'" We were now walking swiftly in the streets of Saint-Germain. People who had read about Jean-Jacques in the papers stared at him in awe. He was more than a movie star in Paris; he was a revolutionary star. His politics were his charismatic crown of trouble, which he wore like a rebel king. Onlookers saw the famous activist Lebel with a young woman in a blue denim jacket and a black T-shirt and sandals running to catch up with him, my long hair soggy on my neck from the heat.

Before I met Jean-Jacques, I had read about him in the *Herald Tribune,* which was printed in English, and also in the French papers, especially *Le Monde,* where he appeared daily in photographs of his demonstrations. He was the French rebel who attracted the beatniks of Paris to his events, his readings, and his political caw-caw-cawing on soapboxes. He attracted the same kind of curiosity seeker who had run to hear Madame de Staël or Robespierre during the French Revolution. Allen Ginsberg—the bearded American poet who screamed about his mother in a madhouse at his poetry readings, where French and American wannabee beatniks applauded this new voice of protest—was often photographed with his lover Peter Orlovsky and Jean-Jacques. I had met Gregory Corso, who followed Lebel around Paris. The sedate William Burroughs, who lived in the "Beat Hotel" in Saint-Germain, was often in attendance at Lebel shows. Brion Gysin, who adopted the Burroughs technique of throwing pages in the air and catching them and letting the accident of chance do the editing, was also a friend and follower of Lebel and appeared at his cyclops events. It was Gysin who had volunteered to create the illustrations for my first book of poems, which was due to come out in a month, published by Two Cities Press. But my future book seemed suddenly distant, and I felt insecure with this red-haired rebel.

As we ran through the streets I asked Lebel whom his favorite philosopher was.

"Believe it or not, I like an old philosopher, Berkeley, who pointed out that all that can ever be experienced by conscious beings is the contents of their consciousness. Nothing else can be known to exist. He was the hippest of all the philosophers. He said, 'Truth is the cry of all but the game of few.' Forget everything Berkeley wrote about God. That was show-off window dressing. Berkeley's genius was that in the seventeenth century he talked about truth, which is what exists in our minds as experience. But now nobody even talks about Berkeley, let alone reads him. All those phonies at the Collège de France are drooling over Hegel and Nietzsche, who led to existentialism, which is nothing but a farcical bullshit philosophy without a sense of humor. Berkeley is the man who led to Tzara and Schwitters and the Dadaists and the surrealists—and for that matter to the stream of consciousness of James Joyce and his magical kabbalah of global language and wordplay, *Finnegans Wake*. Joyce was Irish the way Berkeley was. Oh yes, old James, he took the magic of words and music and syllables and put them together in a madhouse book that was a spit in the face to all those academics and readers of language who never wanted to be challenged by the unconscious or nursery rhymes or wordplay. Joyce is the illegitimate grandson of Berkeley because he gets back to the most primordial archetype of what poetry is, which is the cry of truth that sometimes is so personal it can hardly be understood. But the Dostoyevskys of the world, the Ginsbergs, the Berkeleys, the Joyces of the world, are spitting out their own basic insights. All these artists have something in common: they are literary clowns. Like Henry Miller is a clown. The painters who will be in my barge, Tinguely and Hiquily, are clowns. Picasso is a clown. We must mix up dream and reason to create truth, whatever is in our minds. We have to spit it out. A philosophy of truth is to be aware of your own truth."

Jean-Jacques riffed like a jazz musician, and I felt that twenty-five hundred years of Western philosophy was only an arrow in his bow. His bull's-eye was troublemaking.

As we walked swiftly along the burning sidewalks of Paris, a city that was almost deserted due to the traditional Ferragosto mentality that France and Italy lived by (the August break from the working-day world), I heard the words of Peggy Peterson in my mind, which was now racing with sexual anticipation and was hardly the dispenser of brainwaves of common sense. Peggy had rung me up on the phone in my Montparnasse apartment that morning to say, somewhat archly, "Jean-Jacques is a spoiled rich brat. He's not really an artist. His drawings are considered *merde*. He's a show-off and an attention-grabber with an exalted idea of revolution and changing history. If you want to throw away your life, Sandra, to mount the barricades with him carrying the red flag of revolution, that's your choice. I know how out of place you feel being the rejected wife of Shomsky, who goes off to fiddle while Rome burns, so to speak, but at least you have a commitment from him and have made *some* kind of life. It's so exciting that your first book of poems is going to be published by none other than the legendary Anaïs Nin and Lawrence Durrell. Why don't you consider that to be a door opening for you and stay put in your apartment in Montparnasse until Shomsky returns? You can always have dinner with me at the embassy, because of course I realize how lonely you must be. But don't let your misery with Shomsky push you into the whirlpool of another world where you will, I can assure you, be more miserable. You're still used to a middle-class life and will never fit into a world of drugs and revolution."

I had replied, not very convincingly, "Jean-Jacques doesn't take drugs. Revolution and sex are his drugs."

Peggy shot back, "Well, he may not take drugs, but all the wild men around him do. All those beatnik poets are high all the time, and a lot of them shoot or sniff heroin. Besides, the only thing Lebel will ever commit to is publicity. He's a total publicity freak."

To which I answered, "That's his political tool." She threw me a "big kiss," hung up the phone, and went back to her desk job.

Was Peggy right?

Now it was almost too late for me to turn back, although a part of me wanted to run home and hide under the covers in my warm and safe apartment, which I had decorated so lovingly with silver-framed pictures of Shomsky with many of the world's great violinists. On my kitchen bulletin board I had tacked photographs of Anne Sexton, my favorite woman poet, whom I had met when we were both studying with Robert Lowell at Boston University during a nonresident term. Now, too, there were photographs snapped recently of Pablo and Matilde Neruda. They were next to photographs of my mother and me when I was a child at boarding school, and of Sidney holding me in his arms when I was a little girl and still crazy about my daddy.

Running after Lebel in Paris, I suddenly missed my parents and felt so estranged from them. They had not even a clue as to what my life was like. My father didn't know I was broke all the time, because Shomsky talked a good game, and to listen to his spiel you would have thought he was making a fabulous living performing all over the world. My mother knew from my letters that Shomsky had been honored to be asked to entertain in Cuba and, although she certainly was not a liberal, she still thought it was exciting that he would be appearing with such celebrities as Françoise Sagan and Yves Montand, who were all part of the so-called glamorous Left. My parents didn't know that I felt like an estranged expatriate without a job or career, and that being the wife of the great Shomsky meant constantly being put down by an egomaniac for whom I was a convenience, not a loved one.

My marriage stunk. There was no real camaraderie, very little sex, and the winds of glamour that wafted into my letters home, which were cheerful, were all designed to cover up the fact that I wasn't waving but drowning.

My mother was busy with her teaching and very involved with her second husband and second family, and even though she wrote me loving letters in her beautiful penmanship, I had no real contact with her. She would never accept my collect calls because she was too cheap. I saved my confidences for my father's girlfriend, Aunt Jewel, but even to her I had not told the real truth out of fear that my father would fly to Paris and demand that I return home.

I thought of these things as I entered the dark hallway of Jean-Jacques's building, which was what in New York City we called a townhouse without an elevator. He switched on the light in the hallway. Up we climbed, six flights of stairs to his apartment, which was on the top floor.

"I live with a girl whom I'm about to dump," he said. "So don't be surprised if she's waiting for me."

"You do? For God's sake, what are you doing with me?" I asked.

"Don't be some bourgeois idiot, Sandra. After all, you're married yourself. This girl is some Polish girl who is infected with revolution. She comes from Warsaw, which is communist, and she's what you might call a revolution groupie. She's a good kid and she had nowhere to live."

Just then a very attractive, almost beautiful, black-haired, tall and thin young woman came down the stairs. She was dressed in what looked like a peasant costume. She was carrying a birthday cake with candles that were not lit. You could tell from her fierce eyes that she was freaking out and was furious at Jean-Jacques and jealous of me. Screaming in Polish "*Chinquoya,*" she smashed the cake in Jean-Jacques's face and continued running down the steps, screaming, "*Tak, tak, tak!*"

Jean-Jacques stood still. Whipped cream and chocolate layer cake covered his nose and face while the rest of the cake fell on his clothes. The candles, small and pink, stuck to his fine white-silk polo shirt, which probably cost a fortune and was now ruined. He began to laugh, a loud, grand-inquisitor laugh, like some pauper who had just had a prank pulled on him and suddenly forgot he was supposed to be a pauper. He wiped away the whipped cream with his arm and brushed the cake off his shirt till it fell in curds on the stairway along with the pink candles.

"I guess she got the message," he said matter-of-factly. He continued to climb the stairs. I heard the heavy door on the first floor slam. I followed him, amazed by his cool way of handling the situation.

"Don't worry," he said, opening the door to his apartment with a key. "She didn't like me anymore than I really liked her.

153

She was just some slut I was trying to help out, and she thought she could squat in my apartment for the rest of the summer. Too bad. I hate when things end badly between comrades."

We were now in Jean-Jacques's strange and beautiful environment. A poster of Che Guevara hung on the wall. Candles in crystal candleholders burned that the departing tenant had not bothered to blow out. A huge bed was covered with a deep green velvet bedspread. Dozens of square white pillows were stuffed into freshly starched pillowcases. Since I did all the ironing in my household, I could tell that the king of revolutionaries employed a *femme de chambre*. The apartment was covered with Jean-Jacques's surrealistic drawings, which were made with what seemed like black magic markers. The whole apartment seemed almost like the movie set of an artist's residence. Shoes were arranged neatly in a row in an antique yellow armoire, and the furniture was also antique.

"Like it?" Jean-Jacques asked, surprisingly house-proud. There were a pair of black mesh stockings and a bra—belonging, I guessed, to the furious Polish girl—thrown over a velvet chair. He picked them up and tossed them into an antique wooden wastebasket. "Good-bye, my darlings," he said to the discarded underwear. I was speechless. He excused the luxury of his flat. "All this antique stuff comes from my parents' apartment. They live like kings in Passy, and this is their throw-away junk that I put together when I bought this place last year. It's my haven from the rowdy streets."

I saw that it was part apartment and part painter's studio. Photographs of men I deduced to be Dadaists were framed in gold, and there was a large portrait of Marcel Duchamp standing by some of his found objects. I stared.

"Duchamp is really my favorite philosopher, if you want to know the truth," Jean-Jacques said. "He believes in chance. Everything happens by chance, and that's what makes life a work of art. He thought found objects, like old toilets, were beautiful."

He went into a small kitchen and opened a bottle of red wine, pouring some for me into a large, thick crystal goblet and a glass for himself. He clinked glasses with me. "Here's to great sex," he laughed.

I was already dizzy from the whole experience. He flipped a jazz record of Miles Davis on the gramophone.

It wasn't long before Jean-Jacques and I undressed, almost like children, without embarrassment. I suddenly saw him as some sort of sexual cherub. We practically danced into his large bed, hugging and kissing each other with passionate affection. I felt as if I were in a fairy tale and we had reached a gingerbread house at the end of the woods where there was no witch to watch over us, only the poster of Che Guevara, who smiled a little under his black beret.

"That's what it's all about," Jean-Jacques said. I looked at his full lips and slightly slanted blue eyes. This is what everyone was looking for. This was how to forget we were in the world. This was bliss. Forget everything but unconsciousness together, two as one. Eros is the starter of wisdom. He was now my red-haired satyr and my savior, and I felt our total sexual happiness. I was hooked.

An alarm clock rang, piercing my ears with its shrillness. Jean-Jacques bounded toward me to kiss me and then turned off the clock. "Hey, beautiful!" he screamed. "Wake up! It's my birthday, and we're going to Venice together."

He started throwing jeans and silk T-shirts into a duffel bag that looked more proletarian than anything else in the magnificent apartment.

"Me too?" I asked in bewilderment.

"Of course you too. You're my old lady now."

I got up and felt beautiful because he thought I was. "I have to go back to my apartment and get some clothes," I said.

"Fuck clothes. You're almost my size. You can wear my stuff. You're not going anywhere. We have to catch the train at the Gare Saint-Lazare. It leaves in an hour."

I started to dress and comb my hair with one of his combs, which lay on an antique dresser. "What about my house? Shomsky?"

He looked amazed. "What house? Shomsky who? Forget him. He's history. You're with me now." He was giggling like a schoolboy. "From now on, you're with me, babe."

The Death Barge was to originate from the Galleria il Canale in Milano. The name of the entire event was the Anti-Process (*Anti-procès* in French). It was also called the Manifestazione Collettiva Internazionale. The other two originators of the Anti-Process were the owner of the gallery and the art critic Alain Jouffroy, but Jean-Jacques was the little engine who could, and he was the main organizer.

And that's how I became a comrade-in-arms.

Once on the train, we were installed in a first-class cabin. Jean-Jacques seemed to have wads of francs. Money was not a problem for him because his parents were very wealthy. They were the largest collectors in France of Duchamp paintings and found objects. His father had written a seminal book on Francis Picabia, one of the original Dadaists, and the book was treasured in art circles around the world. Jean-Jacques had been born in Paris, but he'd grown up in Washington, D.C. He told me he had cut his teeth of surrealism on the knee of Max Ernst. You might say he was Dadaist royalty.

"What are you doing?" I asked him. He was sitting across from me on the brown velvet seat, his curly red hair bent over a red leather notebook emblazoned with the letter *C,* which I knew meant it had come from Cartier.

"I'm making a list of some of the artists who are coming to the reading I'm giving at the Milano bookstore that my friend Mario owns. Then we're all going down on the train to Venice, where we will be joined by dozens for the Death Barge demonstration of the Anti-Process."

He read some of the names of the artists who would be protesting with him against the art establishment. Ferro. César. I had heard of Ferro but had never seen his work. The sculptures of César, which consisted of automobiles smashed like tin cans into forms, I was familiar with. César was the darling of the arts reporters of *Le Monde* and the English-language *Herald Tribune*.

"Wifredo Lam, the Cuban painter, of course," Jean-Jacques added. I had seen the work of Lam all over *French Vogue,* to which I had a subscription. Lam was tall and handsome, with coffee-colored skin. He made Picassoesque collages.

"Then, of course, there's Arman," Jean-Jacques said.

"Who is he?" I asked.

"You haven't heard of Arman?" he asked incredulously.

"No."

"He's a great artist born in Nice, whose exhibit of art is going to be held in Paris in the fall. You will definitely get an invitation. The invitations are going to be locked inside anchovy cans that you have to open with the key. The anchovies will be replaced by the invitation."

"How clever," I said.

"And Christo is coming, with his wife," Lebel continued.

Christo, I knew, had married a wealthy French woman, Jeanne-Claude, who was his collaborator and also financed his work, which consisted of wrapping parks and monuments in gauze. He also financed his wrappings of architecture and nature by selling drawings of his proposed wraps in an art gallery. To this band of antiestablishment artists were drawn many of the young rebels of Italy, where Giorgio de Chirico had informed surrealism with its political protest. On the train, I looked at Lebel and thought how much I cared for him.

"I'm going deaf," Jean-Jacques told me quietly. "I'm already deaf in one ear."

"Oh, that's terrible," I said. As the train rocked toward Milano, going *chickachoo, chickachoo, chickachoo, chickachoo,* I had a fantasy that I would go to medical school and study to be an ear doctor, a specialist who could cure Jean-Jacques's deafness and save him from being isolated one day in silence.

I realized that there was a very deep, maternal part of me that wanted to nurture and enable genius, and that once I was sexually involved with a man, my entire persona became wrapped up in being a caretaker. But Jean-Jacques was also a giver, not just a taker like Shomsky. I was learning so much from him about politics and art and courage. He was an entrepreneur of history. Jean-Jacques was CEO of a magical artistic world where change was possible. Instead of following the numbers the way corporate hucksters did, he was involved in anticorporate trickery. Jean-Jacques was a clown of change who could maneuver all the plates that were whirling on sticks and catch them—and then smash them.

I was leaving the world of the musical performer and conductor and patron and was entering the world of political-artistic shakedown and guerrilla-theater performance. Whereas Shomsky often seemed annoyed at me and paid very little attention to what I thought, Jean-Jacques was always asking me questions and sharing with me his radical ideas, thoughts, and strategies. He was the head of the French revolutionary mafia. I looked out the window of the train chugging to Milano and wondered that I was on this exciting journey to a place where I had never been. Jean-Jacques spoke English like an American, French like a Frenchman, and Italian like an Italian. Having never really gone to school formally outside of some diplomatic private school in Washington, he was an autodidact and had a sharp mind without having a sharp tongue.

His voice was low and always even, and the only time he ever showed emotion was when he was demonstrating or reading his manifestos. Otherwise, he was very soft and affectionate, and he demanded that I sit next to him on the train so he could hold my hand or occasionally kiss me. Even his snuggle was erotic.

Finally, we reached Milano. He jumped up and like a little boy yelled, "Yay! We're in the land of Michelangelo and da Vinci and Vivaldi."

We rushed off the train. We were met by Mario Ventelli and a bunch of screaming students, wild men, some wild-looking women, and a collection of Mario's elegant sidekicks.

"Mario is a communist," Jean-Jacques whispered proudly to me, "but he's also for the anarchist revolution. He's just in love with trouble, which is why he's helping to finance the Anti-Process."

I was introduced to everyone, and they were all affectionate and friendly. Mario hugged me, and we rode with Jean-Jacques to our destination, which was Mario's oversized townhouse in the chic section of Milano. I had never met a very rich communist. The building was part bookstore, part living quarters.

Once installed in Mario's townhouse, Jean-Jacques and I were shown to our unbearably beautiful bedroom. It was an enormous room with tiles on the floor the color of brick, ancient Persian carpets over the tiles, a huge bed with a white mosquito-net canopy, and walls the color of newly seeded grass. The walls were covered with avant-garde surrealist pictures mostly by Mario's artist friend Wifredo Lam, as well as gold-framed etchings by Picasso and Daumier. Brown-marble statues from another century were set on Rousseau-green silk pedestals, and a large, lacquered Chinese coffee table was covered with magazines in Spanish, Italian, French, and English. I climbed into the luxurious bed to take a nap while Jean-Jacques pranced into a nearby sitting room, equally luxurious, to talk with Mario. The red-lacquered, thick wooden door separating the two rooms was left slightly open, and I could hear the conversation. Mario and Jean-Jacques talked revolutionary dreams.

"We will, in a few years, be provoking the greatest general strike in history," Mario said quietly. "Your student revolt in Paris will erupt like a volcano. The shock waves will reach every corner of the world." He lit a pipe, and I could hear him puffing on the tobacco.

"We are planning the revolution," Mario continued, "in Paris now, and it will take some time, of course. The Anti-Process is a good beginning. At its height, millions of workers will be on strike. The aftereffects will never truly subside. When that day comes, we will hoist the red flag all over Paris, but now it is time to plan and set up committees. I am so privileged to be funding all this. Every layer of society will be swept along by the tidal wave of change. It will be a break with the past and a flowering of human talent. No one but the artist sees the approach of this great movement, except for a few leaders such as my friend Danilo Dolci, in Sicily. He will join us in change. Thousands will feel its effects, and ruling classes everywhere will tremble at the consequences."

They were drinking now. I could hear them clinking glasses.

"And when the time comes, I will be able to lead this revolution with my crazy friend Danny the Red who is—even now as we speak—laying the foundations. Believe me, fear is not his middle name. He is made up of wire and a certain dark laughter that allows him to play the invisible provocateur. When the student revolt happens, it will seem, however, that it came from nowhere, out of the blue."

Jean-Jacques was now speaking in a soft and conspiratorial voice. "De Gaulle's bullshit of a chromium-plated boom which started last year appears to idiots to seem as if French goods are gaining ground on the world market. Bullshit. He would have the whole of western Europe believe in Voltaire's 'All is for the best in this best of all possible worlds.' Thank you, General Pangloss." The two laughed.

They clinked glasses again. "One day, the unsuspected students will be the leaders," Mario continued. "Anyone who has an intuition of what is happening can see it coming. Frustration toward overcrowded facilities, insensitive administrators in the universities, and of course ineffective learning, procedures that are outdated, the lack of method for students to discuss what is actually happening in Algeria, Cuba, Vietnam. Small student groups are already talking insurrection in cells that nobody knows of. The seeds are there, my friend. A few years from now, the students will be like artists drawing in the dark, and then the lights will go on and there will be broken windows and arrests, and it will make the overthrow of Batista seem like child's play."

"We will finally be in solidarity between the students and workers, and Charles de Gaulle will look like what we call in America a has-been," Jean-Jacques threw in.

"Good. If all goes as planned, Venice will be the beginning."

"I've arranged for the barge," Jean-Jacques said matter-of-factly. "Thank you for the funds, and it's really going to be quite a magnificent thing, to see it going up the canals along with the vaporettos and gondolas. But what about the reading tonight at the bookstore?"

"It's time. Everyone is waiting for you. By the way, who is the girl? I mean, can we trust her?"

"Of course. She's a married poet. I asked her to read with us after the manifestos."

I jumped out of bed and wondered what I would read. I'd had no idea I was going to be part of the bookstore happening.

We found ourselves in what was a huge bookstore and gallery combined. About fifty people were sitting on folding chairs, gabbing and laughing and waiting for us. We marched in like a ragtag army. Then Mario stood in front of the crowd, and there was a hushed silence. He was respected by everyone in Milano, communists and noncommunists, anarchists, and even some older art patrons who were proud of this center of culture in a rather conservative city where industrialists sat bored to death at the opera at La Scala and snoozed while their wives and mistresses paraded up and down the aisles, showing off their Sorelle Fontana outfits and Buccellati jewelry.

The crowd was both chic and plebeian, and anxious for the reading to begin. Sitting in the front row were many of the artists and writers who were going with us the next day to Venice for the Anti-Process. Everyone was looking forward to the event and the ripples it would cause among the wealthy art patrons and dealers who had no idea of what was about to happen on their sacred turf of Venice. The capitalist art market was about to drop. Jean-Jacques stood up and addressed the crowd. He spoke in English, and behind was his double, as it were: a Milanese revolutionary who echoed everything he said in Italian, so that those few in the crowd who didn't really understand English could comprehend what was being said.

"I am Jean-Jacques Lebel," he began humbly, so that he could work his way up to the arrogance of his manifesto slowly. "A few of you have read in the papers about the Anti-Process that we are leading tomorrow against the establishment and all those maniacs that think art is created to be investments for the rich, which it has become, of course."

There was a large surge of catcalls and applause. He began chanting. "In the words of a true artist of the new age, our friend Pablo Picasso, who could not be here tonight but joins us in spirit, 'It is not what the artist does that counts; it is who he is.'"

More applause.

"Picasso has said, and I quote, 'Statues should be put back where they really belong.' Go to the Louvre, for example, drag one of those Egyptian colossi out of its somnolence, and then set it up in the heart of a crowded neighborhood. I can well visualize this king of ancient Egypt placed on the bank of the Saint-Denis Canal, his majestic black silhouette standing out against the yellow sky at the hour when the workmen leave the factories, facing the iridescent waters of the canal in which the factory smoke is reflected. The whole landscape will be changed in a single stroke."

More applause from the crowd. Lebel giggled and continued, now in a louder and more strident voice.

"The whole art world is a hoax. It's all about the dealers and money. It has nothing to do with man's emotions or visions, its trickery and sophistry. And today, as Picasso says, 'Art is a lie.' The dealer despises the artist. The rich people collecting art use art as crank or crystal meth against the boredom and stupidity of their own lives. Art is the cover-up logo that is like the red caps they once made Jews wear in Venice. The collectors go home at night to the ghetto of their own sadness and try to content themselves with the fact that they are buyers of shamans instead of breaking down the ghetto wall and creating revolution. Let us learn from the masters, such as Man Ray, to use humor and mystification as our weapons and tools. It is only through disorder that we again can find order. Let our monuments to humanity suggest the irrational tastes that we know from our dreams. Let our projects be made from all kinds of material used helter-skelter—wood, plaster, a corset, musical toys. Let our monuments move and emit sounds as they do in the sculptures of Tinguely, who is joining us on the Death Barge. Dada, like the true revolution, cannot be pacified. Through its clumsiness, its anxiety and disorganization, Dada is poetry itself, and is stifled by harmony. Finally, in the words of Francis Picabia, 'It is hard to imagine how stupid and tranquil people are made by success.'"

I felt a buzz, a huge shot of energy, something like an epiphany. How marvelous it was to be seated at this reading with students and gurus of the new, with Jean-Jacques as a magus showing the way of the warrior. Jean-Jacques was a link with a world that had vanished, the world of Dada and surrealism, where Tristan Tzara had declared, "There are no mistakes" and "I consider myself very charming."

Lebel was a warrior who did everything childlike to shock the world of the ordinary into truth. In a degenerate man's world of the biosphere where mankind was encouraged to behave like identical dolls or robots stamped from a machine, a world where so many people were slaves wasting their time on trivia, guzzling the last of man's remaining resources, he was young and rebellious but also an archetype of the old soul drawing from the energy of his beliefs to reawaken people with his comic metaphysics, using his powers constructively to ridicule the values of materialistic idiocy. I sat in awe of clown-like insanity and suddenly saw him pointing his chubby little-boy finger at me.

"We have here with us an American poet whose book will soon be published by Anaïs Nin and Two Cities Press in Paris." He looked at me. "Please recite one of your poems for us," he said. "And stand up."

A lot of people turned around to look at me. I got up, and clearly, without any nervousness at all, chanted a poem that would not be in my new book, something I had just written since meeting Jean-Jacques.

ABOUT BLOOD

About blood I've my right hand in the sun
I burn my past my face my name

Oh I have my Godhand at last in the fiery flame
I enter light I shall put on
The tennis sneakers of swift martyrdom
I'll run past palaces and pensiónes
Canals hotels public Italian johns
For this is not the heart of love that feasts
On someone's marriage sheets
Though flesh has held me with its
Featherfingers I am gone
Now I have my right hand in the sun.

I sat down. The tremendous applause made me sweat. The manifesto and reading were over. Students and artsy-looking young boys and girls stacked the folding chairs in piles while everyone gathered in groups for what was now a cocktail party. Mario had set out, on a wooden table covered in silk, wines and liquors and all kinds of crackers, cheeses, black bread, huge bowls of fettuccine with silver tongs that everybody dived into, and melons and prosciutto.

The beatnik poet Gregory Corso appeared like a drunken madman. He ran up to me and gave me the carved head of a angel, which I accepted as a treasured gift and put in the pocketbook slung over my arm.

"I stole that for you. Because you are a brilliant angel," he said and disappeared in the mob.

Jean-Jacques came and kissed me. "The poem was perfect," he said as he moved into a circle of Mario's friends, drinking wine and laughing. The extraordinary painter Manina had also come down from Paris for the reading. She was a stunning older woman in her fifties who had become my new best friend, and that evening she resembled Theda Bara with more than the usual black pencil under her eyes, which were large and blue. She was wearing black fishnet stockings, very high heels, a magnificent black silk dress that showed off her thin figure, and chunky fake diamonds set in silver industrial lava, which she had created in her sculpture studio. Her voice was unforgettable, high-pitched yet sensual. Her beautiful lips were painted with very red lipstick. She wore dark brown enamel on her long fingernails, which was unique for the time. Her hair was a mass of black curls, tinged with gray.

"I see you as the best companion for Jean-Jacques, whose creation of revolution is like a mind-altering drug. Inside of us are archetypes, my dear. Magician, scientist, missionary, domestic goddess, we are all archetypes on an unmarked path. I see from your extraordinary poem that you have chosen to leave the domestic-goddess archetype behind and play the anarchist-revolutionary missionary with Jean-Jacques. That is good."

"I hope so," I said. I was agog with the excitement of this charged atmosphere, which was growing thick with urgent-sounding words in Italian ("*pronto*"), French ("*Vive la révolution*"), and Spanish, droplets of words in every language mixing with the clinking of glasses and drinking of wine.

The poet Corso, like a satyr, ran up to me again and handed me some cheese on brown crackers and then sifted back into the crowd. I thanked him. I was aware that my archetype of good daughter and domestic goddess was now the archetype of the magician's assistant.

As if she could read my mind, Manina said, "You cannot just see Jean-Jacques as a revolutionary fool. A lot of his knowledge comes not only from the Dadaists and surrealists but surprisingly from the mystic philosopher Gurdjieff." Gurdjieff devoted his life to uncovering hidden knowledge, which he called "the work." Gurdjieff was a friend of Jean-Jacques's father before the war. Jean-Jacques told how Gurdjieff went to his parents' house to discuss his quest for knowledge. His father recorded these conversations and often played them for Jean-Jacques. Gurdjieff was considered by Jean-Jacques's father to be the greatest man he had ever met. He was born

166

in Armenia and grew up learning to be tough. He traveled by foot in regions—Central Asia and the Middle East—where an ancient way of life persisted. Manina said, "This old way of life he defined in terms of growth, of being the external practices of various ways of thought, which were secret traditions relating to the transformation of man. To bring together these traditions and unite them into a single system was the self-appointed task of Gurdjieff's seekers of the truth. You should read his remarkable writings." She smiled. I thought of how deeply spiritual she was.

"I'd like to," I said, fascinated by this whole new revelation about Jean-Jacques's mystical education.

"Many attempts have been made to discover the sources from which Gurdjieff collected his knowledge. It appears that some of it came from the Sarmoung brotherhood." She explained that the Sarmoung brotherhood was an esoteric Sufi society based in Asia. Gurdjieff visited their monastery in Kafiristan. Some of his knowledge also came from Tibet, she continued, and some from the Naqshbandi order of dervishes, whose center of activity lay in Bukhara. Other elements seemed to be derived from the Pythagoreans and Rosicrucians of the sixteenth and seventeenth centuries. "We have reason to believe that he also found certain important material in Ethiopia. The man is my *god*," she said mysteriously.

Just then Jean-Jacques joined us. "What are you two girls talking about?" he demanded to know, like a spoiled child who had to be told everything.

"Manina was telling me about how you were influenced by Gurdjieff."

"Bullshit," he said. "Let's get out of here."

"But you were influenced by Gurdjieff," I told him.

"Yeah, I was for a while until I stopped believing in God. Which was when I was about ten years old. But there was a story that my father told me, about Gurdjieff, whom he considered one of the coolest dudes who ever lived. And yeah, I guess I know who he is, but he doesn't interest me at all because he wasn't a revolutionary."

With that, Jean-Jacques burst into laughter and led me out of the throng of partygoers, who were getting drunker and drunker, with Mario making loud toasts in Italian to Jean-Jacques as we left.

We climbed up to the apartment above and dropped on the bed.

"There are future revolutionaries everywhere," Jean-Jacques said.

"I can't wait for tomorrow," I said, turning to give him a hug, hoping he didn't think I didn't appreciate the most exciting evening of my life.

Riding on the train to Venice, Jean-Jacques was like a young general leading a drunken army. The cars of the train were filled with Mario, his Italian friends, his family, and his band of artists and protestors. Jean-Jacques had a flask of bourbon and was drinking from it in intervals. Everyone else was also drinking. Suddenly Jean-Jacques looked depressed, like a child suffering a panic attack. "What if all the press doesn't come out and nobody sees us?" he asked.

"Impossible," I said to bolster his spirits.

"The media is our weapon," he said and then fell asleep.

I sat on the velvet throne of the train, looking at the passing scenery, and wondered what I had gotten myself into. I also felt a strange sadness. I was trying to find my path in life. Should I be a mother? A wife? A revolutionary? A poet? A student who would one day be an academic? A mystic? It was confusing to be a revolutionary, because again I was a sidekick. Other than Manina and myself, no women were part of Jean-Jacques's movement—and, come to think of it, there were not many female Dadaists either. Yet I had to push myself to do something uncomfortable with my life, and perhaps I could inspire Jean-Jacques and be part of his movement for liberation.

I tried to put my guilt out of my mind. Shomsky had no idea where I was. There was a certain thrill in running away. But where was I running to? What was the purpose of life, anyway? To warm my soul? To warm someone else's soul? To breed? To change humanity? Was Jean-Jacques the soul glue that I needed? And hadn't the fact that I didn't have a real family life, a home—that I had never had a home after my parents' divorce—tell me that *that* was what I wanted? Did I want to shock my parents? I knew that my parents would be frightened for my revolutionary future if they knew what I was doing. I knew that my life was as brief as a meteor streaking across the sky. And I had to make the most of every moment. I thought how lucky I was to know all these artists who could express the dimensions of their creativity with brushes and clay and paint and demonstrations.

As soon as we arrived in Venice, Jean-Jacques shepherded me to a small hotel called Montin, located on Giudecca, an island near Venice. The ride in the gondola was exciting. I saw the city that I had not seen since I was fifteen and had gone on a tour of Europe as a boarding school student. The palazzos were domed ancient remembrances of what Venice had been centuries ago. Plastered all over the city were huge posters announcing the Biennale. Jean-Jacques had done his work. There were also posters announcing the Anti-Process.

Montin was a hole in the wall. We went immediately to the bar, which led out to a sunny courtyard where people were pleasuring themselves by enjoying a long and delicious Italian lunch. Over the bar hung paintings, etchings, and watercolors by famous artists. There were many by the American artists de Kooning, Robert Indiana, Andy Warhol, Jasper Johns, and dozens of others who had stayed at the hotel.

"Here at Montin, the artists pay with paintings. Isn't that great? No charge for us, sweetheart," Jean-Jacques cried. I could see some of his own creations made with black magic markers on the wall. "See? I'm famous!"

Jean-Jacques was a king at Montin. All the waiters knew him, and Montin himself came out to greet him in a white apron. They hugged, macho-style. A maid took us to our room. It was large and covered with paintings by Spanish, French, and Italian contemporary artists. There was a huge bed and a large mirror in an ornate gold frame covering one of the walls. Jean-Jacques took off his clothes. He began to jump naked on the bed.

"Come on, sweetheart, jump with me!"

I took off my clothes and began jumping as if the bed were a trampoline.

"Yeee!" Jean-Jacques screamed in delight.

He was admiring his naked body. "Isn't this a beautiful cock?" he asked. "Look. Look."

We stared at ourselves jumping for joy on the bed.

"The body is so beautiful!" I screamed. We were already high on a sort of sexual glee, which was the helium of our revolutionary experience.

"Hurry up. Let's make love," he demanded in a childish way.

We stopped jumping and lay down in the bed. We made love and Jean-Jacques began drinking from his flask.

"Get dressed. I have a surprise," he said.

We put our clothes on again. He ran down the stairs, with me following him, out into the sunlight. The hotel was on a canal. Jean-Jacques jumped into the canal. He was drinking and happy and wet.

"Come on!" he screamed. "Jump!"

"With my clothes on?"

"Sure!"

I jumped into the canal. Garbage was floating in the water, rinds of oranges, old flowers. We hugged and splashed around. We were children splashing each other.

"I'm so happy!" I shouted, and for the moment I was happy. For the moment.

Soon Jean-Jacques got out of the water, and we went back to our room to rid our bodies of all the grease and garbage. He dressed in fresh clothes, and so did I, toweling myself dry with enormous white terry-cloth towels from the hotel.

Jean-Jacques went into his executive mode. "The barge is ready. In an hour, we board."

We went quickly down the steps to find the Death Barge. I kept thinking of Rimbaud's poem "The Drunken Boat."

The barge was docked at one of the canals. People were boarding. Some carried banners ("Death to the Dealers") others huge placards: "Art Is Not Meant for Walls" or "No Art in Museums" or "Take Art Back." Some of the passengers were noisy, some drinking. There were dozens of us, some well known, others not at all. Gregory Corso came aboard, screaming, "This is so cool!" Some old man in bathing trunks had a portable radio blaring the *Marseillaise*. People were yelling, eating, dancing, waving protest flags.

The barge took off. Down the canals of Venice we sailed. Hundreds of people watched this shouting mob of protesters. Cameras flashed like lightning bugs on the banks of the canal.

"Death, death, death to the dealers!" everyone chanted.

For hours we sailed in the first revolutionary protest that had ever been staged at the Biennale. Crowds gathered everywhere. Policemen controlled the crowds. There were screams. Media madness. Hype. And the barge was a great success.

Once the revolutionary boat had floated up the canal, all Venice was agog over the protest. A tall, gay man surrounded by artists invited us to his palazzo. It was filled with treasures: icons, Buddhist art from Nepal, pictures in silver frames. His name was Alan and he was one of the instigators of the Death Barge. At his magnificent digs, many artists, all male, were getting drunk. Everybody forgot about me and gathered around Jean-Jacques, who promptly forgot me too. As they got drunker and drunker, Jean-Jacques indicated to me that perhaps it would be better if I went back to the hotel and got some sleep. "Jean-Jacques, you're just like Shomsky: you ignore me. First you take me, but then you ignore me. Fuck you. I want to be where the action is." Everyone was waiting for the papers to come out with headlines about the protest. It seemed a little bit like producers and actors in a Broadway show waiting for the reviews.

In the starry, hot night, I walked by myself through the magnificent city, watching the silent gondolas moving like black birds through the dark waters. I knew Jean-Jacques was living out his dreams, but it dawned on me that his passion was not for me, but for the revolution. I was a sidekick. I went back to our hotel room and began to cry.

The phone rang. It was a long-distance call from America. I heard my father yelling on the phone.

"I had to call the fucking American embassy to track you down in Venice!" he cried. "It seems some cockamamie friend of yours lied and said to the ambassador she had no idea where you were, and then a moment later admitted that you had run off to Venice with some revolutionary. Is that true?"

"Yes."

"Well, let me give you some bad news. You happen to be married, in case you don't know it. And it's been on all the radios that Shomsky was arrested in Cuba two days ago. Shomsky managed to get through to me from jail. Just as a joke, he had taken off his shoes and socks during some kind of rally. The Cuban police happen to be very suspicious and conservative, and even though Shomsky, who's a first-class idiot, tried to explain it was some kind of joke, it seems they're very—what do you call it—homophobic, and they thought he was stripping or something, and they threw him in the clinker. He'd still be rotting there if I hadn't used all my influence in Washington to get him out. It's only because he's your husband; otherwise I couldn't give a shit. Anyway, he's now on his way back to Paris, and I want you to get your ass on a train and get back there as soon as you can. He says he still loves you, and he made a mistake leaving you behind. Whatever happens in the future, I don't need more tsuris and phone calls in the middle of the night. Go home now, and you better listen to me."

I paused. "Daddy, I'm having a good time. I don't want to go home."

"You better. This could hit the papers, and I don't need you embarrassing me. I'm already embarrassed to be your father. *Oy vey,* what a disaster. It's a good thing I found you. I love you!" he shouted as he banged down the phone.

I threw my clothes into my suitcase and left the hotel. At the train station, having taken a vaporetto out of Venice, I immediately found a train that was leaving for Milano and Paris. I was on it.

I awaited for Shomsky to arrive in Paris. The writer Françoise Sagan came to visit me and was concerned about Shomsky. She told me he had been horsing around and suddenly, having delivered a great concert to ovations, he was whisked off to jail. She tried to assure me that he was going to be all right. She seemed to have some sort of crush on my husband and asked me all sorts of questions that seemed more like prying than concern. But she was proud of the fact that she had been chosen to go to the Cuba Libre celebration.

A day later, Shomsky showed up, cursing his beloved Castro and saying that the Cuban police were worse than Nazis. He was horrified to hear that I had gone off to the Biennale with Lebel. He demanded to know if I'd had an affair with him. I lied and told him no, of course not, that it was just something I felt would be fun to do.

The papers in France had covered the event. I was in all the pictures with Lebel hugging me. I had to tell my husband Lebel was gay so he wouldn't be suspicious of our "hot" affair. I let a few weeks pass, and things went back to normal. Shomsky began practicing again. The name Jean-Jacques was never mentioned, but one day I received a postcard from him, still in Venice, that had a huge pornographic cock on it. I knew he had hoped Shomsky would find it, and that it was his way of getting his revenge on me for departing without even leaving a note. The postcards began arriving every day, but since Shomsky never collected the mail (that was one of my jobs), I just kept throwing them out. One postcard read, "I miss fucking you in the ass." I turned beet red and burned it. Jean-Jacques was a provocateur, and even though he showed not the slightest interest in me after we jumped in the canal, forgetting me for the slogan-filled hysteria of the Death Barge, I'm sure he had felt rejected. I was supposed to be his "old lady," his "chick."

I looked forward to the book-signing party for my first book of poems, *Voyage Home,* which Anaïs Nin was hosting at the English bookstore. Shomsky refused to go.

"Because when you married me, you knew I was a concert violinist, and it was your job to be my wife. I'm the one who's supposed to be the star. Going to your book-signing party would make me feel like Mr. Hochman. Besides, all this happened so quickly while I was away. What do you have to publish a book for anyway? To show off?"

"Because I'm a writer."

"You're Madame Shomsky."

"Why can't I be both? How can you be so old-fashioned?"

"I just wouldn't feel comfortable standing around while everyone is paying attention to you."

"Well, if you loved me so much, you'd be proud of me."

"First of all, it's a book you wrote in college, and it has love poems in it that weren't even written to me."

"So what?"

"I don't want to stand around while you're signing books with love poems to someone else."

"They were written when I was twelve, for God's sake, to a boy I had a crush on in boarding school. Why can't you just come? It will be so humiliating for me if you don't show up."

"I don't know Anaïs Nin. I hear she swings both ways. I don't know this Lawrence Durrell either. I won't know anyone there. I'll feel out of place."

"Fuck you. I don't know a lot of people in your concert world, but I tag along anyway because I'm proud of your music. And I even look ridiculous carrying your violin case."

"I won't go."

"Why? If it makes me happy."

"A lot of people will probably ask me about the whole Cuban disaster. It was in all the papers. How did I know that Castro, who's such a revolutionary, was crazy? I was just taking off my shoes and socks as some kind of joke, and they thought I was a fag taking off my clothes in public. I truly tried to say I was joking and I'm not some kind of fairy or drag queen and it was hot so I was taking off my shoes and socks to cool my feet—when these guards grabbed me. My God. Such a macho society. I hate Castro now. If it weren't for your father's influence, I'd be rotting in prison with the other fairies for the rest of my life. That's at least one good thing your old man did for me, even if he is a cheap bastard. But trust me, I don't want to explain the whole thing in public."

"But don't you know how important this book is to me, Shomsky? It's my first book."

"So go by yourself. You don't need me. You're going to be the one everyone talks to. You didn't write it under my name, you wrote it under the name of Hochman."

"That's my maiden name, and I've kept it as my pen name. I began publishing when I was fifteen, long before I knew you."

"Well, I'm only interested in Shomsky events. Not Hochman events. You're nothing but a child trying to find yourself."

"What's wrong with that?"

"I thought you were more mature than you are."

"You're supposed to be my husband, and my brother, and my friend."

"Well, maybe I'm jealous. To be honest, I don't want a woman who is a star where I have to be in her spotlight. I am the star."

"That's the first honest thing you've said. You *are* jealous of me. Of my youth. And of my life. You only want me for yourself. Remember the Cocteau episode? I'll never forget it." I remembered that Shomsky was simply unable to love anyone but himself.

"I won't go," he repeated.

"Then you can forget about my staying married to you."

"Don't threaten. What would you really be without me? A nobody. Your old man won't give you a dime."

"Is money so important to you?"

"Only when you don't have any."

Just as we were arguing, the doorbell rang. It was Shomsky's old friend the film director Jules Dassin. They had been friends for years. Jules was blacklisted in Hollywood and couldn't get work, and we saw him and his girlfriend, Melina

Mercouri, quite often. Dassin was pissed at Shomsky for the Cuba episode.

"Don't answer it," Shomsky said. "It's Dassin. He's very pro the revolution, and he's going to want to know why the hell I fucked up and made a fool of myself, and I don't feel like talking to him about it."

"I thought you were such good friends."

"We were."

"Listen, Shomsky, I think you're reacting in a crazy way. I love you even if you don't come with me to the book signing. If you don't want to go, I'll go alone. Or I'll go with Harold Norse."

"That little creep? Can't you find someone else to be your companion other than that dwarf? I notice he used my shaving cream, my razor, and ran off with some of my socks while he was babysitting you."

"So what? He was kind to me."

"Well, I don't want him around here. Nor do I want Anaïs Nin. And after the Cuban disaster, I'm fed up with commies, so you can make sure Neruda and his hifalutin wife, who always wears gloves, don't come here either. In fact, the whole poetry thing bores me. So go alone."

And so I did.

I loved signing my own book. During the event, Jean-Jacques Lebel came striding in out of nowhere with a big grin and bought twenty-five books and asked me to sign them. He began apologizing for the way he had behaved to me in Venice. He was no longer in his revolutionary mode but actually seemed calm. He was still hoping I'd come back to him.

"I'm proud of you," he said. And I knew he loved me for who I was. "I need you," he whispered to me.

"Do you think love is need?" I asked.

"I don't know what love is," he said. "I had a few laughs with you."

"Love is so short, forgetting is so long," I answered. I was quoting Neruda. But Lebel didn't know that, because he never read Neruda's poetry. To him, Neruda was just a well-known communist. He had no idea that Neruda was the greatest poet of the twentieth century—and that he was my mentor and friend.

At the book signing, I was amazed that fifty of my books, out of the printing of two hundred, sold immediately. Anaïs Nin beamed as if I were her own child. I could hardly believe that I was signing my book—to Allen Ginsberg, Henry Miller, James Jones, James Baldwin, and so many others. I felt alive for the first time.

After the party, it was a starry night and I walked with Harold to a café. "Let's have a drink," I said.

"I have tragic news for you," he said. "You're now as much a bona fide poet as I am. For the rest of your life, when people ask you what you do, you're going to be honest and say, 'I'm a poet,' and they will tell you until you die, 'But I don't understand poetry' or 'Poetry is one thing I never got into,' and they will sneer, unless they are writers themselves, and then they think, 'How pathetic.'"

"I know," I said. There were tears in my eyes. "I have to tell you a secret, Harold."

"Tell me."

"This morning I woke up, and I had an epiphany. A real revelation. All this year in Paris I have been wondering: Who am I? And what am I going to do with my life? And now I know. I'm going to help other writers to get published like Anaïs is helping me."

"Do you know how lucky you are? Do you know how many cocks I had to suck to get my first book published?" Harold said.

"I'm lucky to be in Paris and know you, Harold. I love Paris. At first when I arrived with Shomsky, I felt it was my mission to be a fabulous wife and help him achieve stardom again as a violinist with the great orchestras of the world. Then, as I sensed that he was cheating on me and using me as a prop for his career, I thought my mission was to run off with René Leibowitz and be his muse and give him back his youth and devote myself to atonal music and our life together. When he betrayed me, I ran home for a while, but Paris was tattooed into my skin and I knew I had to return. When Shomsky dumped me to be a big shot and made it clear that I was only a drag and went off to Cuba, I met you, and you changed my life. Anaïs Nin became, out of the goodness of her heart, my enabler. She passed on the torch of being an artist, as she did to so many others. And now I know who I am and what I will be. I woke and felt a light around me, and I heard a voice inside my brain as I woke, and it really was an epiphany. Who am I? I'm going to be a warrior and a writer. Because a writer is always a warrior. But more than that, I'm going to be like Anaïs Nin. I'm going to be an enabler and help other artists. I'll write plays and help actors, I'll make films and help filmmakers, I'll teach children, and my life won't just be living for myself. And that's why, Harold, I'm going back to America for good."

"Take me with you," Harold said. He had tears in his eyes too. And I understood that even though he was queer, he was the only man who had ever *really* loved me. And I knew that of all my affairs, this man who was a vagrant but wrote beautiful lines from his soul would always be my best friend. He looked so sad because he thought we were saying good-bye.

"Of course you can come with me," I said.

Harold smiled and recited the line from his first book that I will always remember: "If you want to survive I would not recommend love."

I miss little Harold who died without ever being recognized as a great poet. This memoir honors him because like so many others in Paris, he changed my life.